ENGLAND IN TRANSITION

Life and Work in the Eighteenth Century

M. DOROTHY GEORGE

Routledge
Taylor & Francis Group
LONDON AND NEW YORK

First published in 1931 by George Routledge & Sons, Ltd.

This edition first published in 2026
by Routledge
4 Park Square, Milton Park, Abingdon, Oxon OX14 4RN

and by Routledge
605 Third Avenue, New York, NY 10158

Routledge is an imprint of the Taylor & Francis Group, an informa business

British Library Cataloguing in Publication Data
A catalogue record for this book is available from the British Library

ISBN: 978-1-032-97576-4 (Set)
ISBN: 978-1-041-14031-3 (Volume 12) (hbk)
ISBN: 978-1-041-14032-0 (Volume 12) (pbk)
ISBN: 978-1-003-67272-2 (Volume 12) (ebk)

DOI: 10.4324/9781003672722

Publisher's Note
The publisher has gone to great lengths to ensure the quality of this reprint but points out that some imperfections in the original copies may be apparent.

Disclaimer
The publisher has made every effort to trace copyright holders and would welcome correspondence from those they have been unable to trace.

ENGLAND IN TRANSITION

SAINT GEORGE FOR ENGLAND

Behold your Saint with Glorious English Fare,
Noble Sirloin, Rich Pudding and Strong Beer.
For you my Hearts of Oak for your Regale,
Here's good old English Stingo Mild and Stale.

This Porter is by Famous Calvert made
Justly Renown'd of all the Brewing Trade,
Such cheer as this will make you Bold and Strong
Who'd not on such a Noble Saint, Rely On.

[*Frontispiece*

ENGLAND IN TRANSITION

LIFE AND WORK IN THE
EIGHTEENTH CENTURY

BY

M. DOROTHY GEORGE

Litt. D., Author of *London Life in the Eighteenth Century*
England in Johnson's Day

LONDON
GEORGE ROUTLEDGE
& SONS, LTD.
1931

NOTE

THIS book is based on a series of broadcast talks given in 1930, and I have to acknowledge the kind permission of the B.B.C. to publish them. But, as a matter of fact, the talks have been so much expanded and re-written as to be almost unrecognisable.

M. D. G.

Printed in Great Britain at
The Mayflower Press, Plymouth. William Brendon & Son, Ltd.

CONTENTS

LIST OF ILLUSTRATIONS

CHAPTER I

OLD ENGLAND—A GOLDEN AGE ?

THE early part of the eighteenth century has something of the glamour of Arcadia. We think of it as the last age of old England, of solid, stable, rural England : the last age before invention, the machine and the factory made the country industrial instead of mainly agricultural. It was a breathing-space before the Industrial Revolution—perhaps the greatest revolution in history. This is one way of looking at it, not without truth. But historians are fighting shy of the term ' Industrial Revolution '—it has been worked too hard, it says too much and too little. Capitalistic industry and even industrialization began long before the middle of the eighteenth century. And in the nineteenth much of old rural England with its scattered industries survived—there are relics of it even now. Life and industry are too richly varied and confused to submit themselves to the generalizations of the writers of history. And the scene changes as the point of view changes.

But from many aspects it is of course true that the middle years of the eighteenth century are a watershed dividing old England from the modern world as we know it. The changes of those decades would be easier to estimate if we had a clearer notion of the state of things before those changes happened. Unfortunately, we know comparatively little about social conditions at the end of the seventeenth and beginning of the eighteenth centuries. We know that there was a very serious problem of poverty. Parliament repeatedly tried to tackle it by laws regulating the granting of poor relief and the punishment of vagrancy—with small success—witness the rapid succession of Acts, the groans of ratepayers and the complaints of pamphleteers. But poverty was taken for granted: as Francis Place remarked: "There was not then the same disposition to pry into the state of society."

Nevertheless people were beginning to pry into the state of society though the attitude of mind was different from that which governed later investigations. At the end of the seventeenth century one of the signs that England was becoming 'modern' was the beginning of the study of statistics or political arithmetic as it was then called. John Graunt, Sir William Petty, Charles Davenant and Gregory King are the fathers of the science. King made an estimate of the population and of the incomes of the various classes of the community "calculated for the year 1688" which has been much used by historians from Macaulay onwards. His figures must be the basis of any estimate of social conditions at the end of the seventeenth century, and they are deeply interesting and illuminating, remote as they are from modern standards of accuracy. He based his calculations on the taxation returns and especially on those of the hated hearth tax. So far as population goes, his estimate of about 5½ millions for England and Wales has been strikingly confirmed by later investigations.

King's estimate of the income of different classes is startling, and perhaps the most startling thing about it is that to his contemporaries there was nothing surprising in his figures. More than half the population, he calculated, were "decreasing the wealth of the kingdom," that is, their expenses exceeded their earnings, and the deficiency had to be made up from poor relief, charity or plunder. His calculations are based on 'families,' or households—at one end of the scale is the peer's 'family' of forty persons, which would include all his indoor servants, not excepting his chaplain; at the other end is the vagrant with no family at all. The phrase 'decreasing the wealth of the kingdom' is itself significant of the point of view, for though it may fairly be given to the vagrant, its application to the labouring man whose utmost efforts cannot support a wife and family at the then rate of wages beg a great many questions.

This submerged or 'unprofitable' majority, dependent in varying degrees on the charity of the nation (2,795,000 out of a total of 5,500,500 persons), included whole classes: "labouring people and out-servants," 364,000 families averaging 3½ persons or 1,300,000 souls; 400,000 families (or 1,300,000 souls) of 'cottagers and paupers'; 50,000 families of common seamen, and 35,000 families of common soldiers making together 220,000 souls. These are the classes which the eighteenth century lumped together as 'the labouring poor.' Only such children as lived with their parents are counted in these families—others swell the total of the families of 'gentlemen,' 'freeholders,' 'farmers,' etc., in whose households they lived as servants. The total of these 'decreasing the wealth of the kingdom' is made up by 30,000 vagrants.

Poverty was also the lot of many who do not appear in this submerged part of the nation. Throughout the eighteenth century there is evidence of the hard life of the small farmer, struggling with the alternate evils of bad seasons and bad markets. Gregory King estimates the farmers at 150,000 families—750,000 persons with an average family income of £44 and an expenditure of £42 10s. The more fortunate freeholders are 180,000. The income of the farmers was less, and their standard of living considerably lower, than that of shopkeepers, tradesmen and artisans.[1]

Luckily, King's figures are illustrated and borne out in a striking way by a pamphlet written about the same time by Richard Baxter (the author of the *Saints' Rest*), but only recently discovered and printed. Its title speaks for itself: *The Poor Husbandman's Advocate to Rich, Racking Landlords*. It gives a vivid picture of the distresses of the small farmer—and according to Baxter by far the greater number of farmers in all counties were small men: "where there is one of 80 or 70 or 60£ [rent]" there are "many of 30 or 20 or 10 or 5£."

[1] See Appendix.

Their lot, he says, is harder than that of their own servants, whose case, " could they but containe themselves from marriage [an important qualification] is farre easyer than of the poor Tenants that are their Masters. For they know their work and wages and are troubled with no cares for paying Rents, or making good Markets, or for the loss of corn or cattle, the rotting of sheepe or the unfavourable weather, nor for providing for wife and children and paying labourers and servants wages." Baxter does not pity them for their hard fare, so long as they have food which is not injurious to health; his chief concern is with their souls—their poverty is so great and their labour so unremitting that they " cannot have time to read a chapter in the Bible or to pray in their families;" very many of them indeed cannot read.

But he does give a striking picture of their way of life: " The poor tenants are glad of a piece of hangd bacon once a week and some few that can kill a Bull eate now and then a bit of hangd beefe enough to trie the Stomack of an ostrige. He is a rich man that can afford to eat a joint of fresh meat (bief, mutton or veale) once in a month or fortnight. If their sow pigge or their hens breed chickens, they cannot afford to eate them but must sell them to make their rent. They cannot afford to eate the eggs that their hens lay, nor the apples or pears that grow on their trees (save some that are not vendible) but must make money of all. All the best of their butter and cheese they must sell, and feed themselves and children and servants with skimd cheese and skimd milke and whey curds." (It is to be noted that this description would apply very fairly to the small-holders in many parts of Europe to-day.) But he adds "through God's mercy all this doth them no harme." He is more concerned with their subjection to their landlords and their landlords' servants: "the poor tenant taketh every foot-boy or groome or porter of his landlord to be a gentleman whose favour seemeth a preferment to him." He deplores the ignorance of religion of "the Enslaved husbandmen." "I may well say *enslaved* for none are so servilely dependent (save household servants and ambitious expectantes) as they are on their landlords. They dare not displease them lest they turn them out of their houses or increase their rents."

Baxter allows many exceptions to this picture of poverty. He is careful to say that he speaks not of all farmers but only of the "rackt poor," who are the more numerous. Near London there are rich farmers who in remote counties would rank as gentlemen. Near other large towns such as Bristol, where there is much demand for their produce, farmers may thrive. Nor does he speak of those who own freehold land besides their farms, nor of those who have some trade by which they may more easily pay their rent: "who have some small tenement of 5£ or 10£ per annum and have besides a trade as a weaver, a butcher, a taylor, a joiner, a carpenter." He is speaking of the small farmer cultivating the land on the old system in common fields.

Baxter compares the farmer's lot with that of the artisan: "It is much easyer with the handicrafte labourer that hath a good trade. A joyner or a turner can worke in the dry house with tolerable and pleasant worke and knoweth his price and wages. A weaver, a shoemaker or a taylor can worke without the wetting or the tiring of his body and can thinke and talke of the concernes of his soule without impediment to his labour. . . . And though the labour of a smyth be hard, it is in a dry house, and but by short fittes, and little, in comparison of Thrashing and Reaping, but as nothing in comparison to the mowing which constantly puls forth a man's whole strength." He goes on to the less fortunate workers: The carrier's work is toilsome and done in all weathers, but he "knoweth his work and wages and is free from the abundance of the toils and cares." The same is true of the domestic workers in iron of the Midlands: "The nailors, and spurryers [spurmakers] and sithsmiths [scythe-smiths] and swordmakers and all the rest about Dudley and Stourbridge and Brummicham [Birmingham] and Walsall and Wedgbury [Wednesbury] and Wolverhampton and all that country. They live in poverty, but not in the husbandman's case: they know their work and wages and have but little further care." This is a most interesting snapshot of the domestic workers round Birmingham and Walsall who worked at their own smithies for merchants and middlemen, as indeed the nailors and chain-makers did till recently.[1] Then as later they lived in poverty, but to Baxter their lot was better than that of the farmer because they were less servilely dependent on landlords, less at the mercy of wind and weather.

To go back to King and his figures. The farmer, with his income of £8 15s. a head for his household

[1] A few hand-made nails are still made in little smithies.

(as compared with the artisan's £10) and an expenditure of £8 10s., poor as he was, yet belongs to the prosperous minority of the nation which is self-supporting. The farmers are far better off than the cottagers and paupers. The income per head of their small households averaging $3\frac{1}{4}$ souls is £2 with an expenditure of £2 10s., to the extent of ten shillings a head a year, so that King regards him as "decreasing the wealth of the nation." And there are 400,000 families of cottagers and paupers and only 150,000 farmers' families.

Davenant found King's figures "very accurate" and "more to be relied upon than any thing that has ever been done in the like kind." Incidentally, he illustrates the technical meaning at that time of the word cottage, namely, a small house or hovel with little or no land. Elizabeth passed a famous Act forbidding the building of houses without at least four acres of land. Some modern writers have interpreted this as meaning that all cottages were to have at least four acres of land. But the title of the Statute is "An Act against the erecting and maintaining of cottages," and its object, as expressed in the preamble, is "for the avoiding of the great inconvenciencies which are found to grow by the creating . . . of great numbers and multitudes of cottages."[1] A dwelling with at least four acres of land (whether in strips in the common fields or enclosed) would cease to be a cottage in the technical sense. Bacon, in the early seventeenth century, speaks of "mere cottagers which are but housed beggars." There was then little or no regular employment for day-labourers on the farms, and so, except in industrial or seafaring places, cottager and pauper were apt to be synonymous terms. The Act made an exception for cottages for industrial workers in specified occupations, game-keepers and seafaring people. It also allowed cottages for the impotent poor to be built on the village waste, with the consent of the lord of the manor and the parish officers. Other cottages might be licensed by the justices in Quarter Sessions, and much of the business of the Sessions in the seventeenth century was taken up by the pressing question of cottages, with ordering their demolition or sanctioning their erection, always as a measure connected with poor relief and the parish poor. For instance, in 1663 the Worcestershire Quarter Sessions sent out circular letters to the justices: "Having at this time received

[1] This Act was similar in intention to the measures for preventing building in London. See Acreage, *London Life*, 60–72.

from all parts of the County divers certificates or presentments of the great number of cottages lately erected, we do with all thankfulness acknowledge your great care and regard of the County therein, it being a work of as great concernment as any we know, for the great neglect that of late has been of this particular has caused this county to abound with poor more than any County in England that we know of."[1]

Davenant shows how King arrived at his deplorable total of 400,000 families of cottagers and paupers: By the returns of the Hearth Tax, out of 1,300,000 houses, 554,000 were houses with one hearth only. But since some of these might have land attached to them, King computed the families of cottagers as 500,000 only. And since some of the 500,000 might be self-supporting and not chargeable to the parish, "Mr. King," says Davenant, "very judiciously computes his cottagers and paupers decreasing the wealth of the nation but at 400,000 families." This to Davenant was a conservative estimate.

Davenant is concerned with the lot of this submerged, not tenth, but more than half, of the

[1] Hist. MSS. Comm., *MSS. in various collections*, i, 1904, Ap. 29, 1663.

nation. He pointed out that they were not immune from taxation. Some duties though to a slight extent, because of their small consumption, reached even to them. These were the taxes on malt, leather and salt. But they felt, he said, the burden of taxation on other classes, since if the gentry were heavily taxed they would neither be able to help nor employ these poor people, nor would the manufacturers be able to pay them so well for carding and spinning: "If the gentry upon whose woods and gleanings they live, and who employ them to day labour, and if the manufacturers for whom they card and spin are overburthened with duties," they could neither pay so well, "nor yield them those other reliefs which are their principal subsistence, for want of which these miserable wretches must perish with cold and hunger." Such remarks show that these cottagers and paupers were not drones but the ill-paid and under-employed.

The figures and comments of King, Davenant and Baxter are a point of departure from which to regard the eighteenth century scene.

The early eighteenth century was a prosperous time. The population was growing slowly, trade was growing fast, and the growth of towns increased the profits of neighbouring farmers. The growth of trade increased the demand for the carding and spinning which gave work to the wives and children of small farmers, labourers and cottagers. Wages were rising in most places. Corn was cheap in the first half of the century, and if this was bad for landlords and farmers it was good for labourers and cottagers and artisans. This is the time which is regarded as the golden age of the agricultural labourer. The standard of living was rising and there is every reason to believe that things improved considerably for almost all classes. But there were exceptions. It became less easy for the destitute family to scrape a livelihood off the land. Their great resource had been squatting on commons, keeping geese, cutting wood and turf, and eking out a living, some by occasional day labour, others by sheep-stealing and poaching. These are the people who were aimed at, both in Elizabeth's Act against cottages and by the famous or notorious Act of Settlement of 1662 which restricted the movement of all those who were not freeholders and could not afford to rent a tenement of £10 a year. "By some defects of the law," said the Act, "poor people are not restrained from going from one parish into another and, therefore do endeavour to settle themselves in those parishees where there is the best stock, the largest commons or wastes to build cottages, and the most woods for them to burn and destroy; and when they have consumed it, then to another parish and at last become rogues and vagabonds. . . ." These were some of Gregory King's class of cottagers and paupers who were "decreasing the wealth of the nation."

But many of this class rose into the ranks of self-supporting day-labourers, small-holders and artisans. No one ever again ventured to suggest that more than half the population was dependent on poor-relief or charity. Although, as commons and heaths were enclosed, forests and marshes were drained, it grew more difficult to live on the land with a minimum of work, many squatters on the waste were able to carve out small holdings for themselves though they were always regarded with a jealous eye by those with rights of common. At the same time there was an increasing demand for spinning and carding which gave employment to women and children in many places.

The freeholders or yeomen are an exception to the general increase in prosperity. The very things which improved the lot of labourers and artisans

—cheap food, rising wages and a rising standard of living and flourishing trade—were in some ways against the small freeholder. Fortunes were being made in trade; the successful merchant nearly always bought land and commenced country gentlemen. Often indeed he was the younger son of a country gentleman who had been apprenticed in the City. It was a general ambition in England to own land, the chief source of social consideration and political influence. This made the price of land higher than its economic value justified. Moreover, the cheap corn of the early eighteenth century meant hard times for farmers and their complaints were persistent. The freeholder was doubly tempted to sell his land and try his fortune in trade.

King had estimated the number of freeholders of the better sort—those with average incomes of £84 a year—as 40,000, while the 'lesser freeholders' with £55 a year were 140,000. These were a recognised social class—below the ranks of 'esquires' and 'gentlemen' and 'clergy' who from the landholding and political point of view were also freeholders. In 1780 it was estimated that the number of freeholders who could vote for knights of the shire was 130,000. At the beginning of the nineteenth century Colquhoun estimated the number of freeholders as 160,000, adding, "There are certainly more freeholders than those stated as such, since, in the present times, every person who is in any degree opulent is also of this class." These figures do not suggest a wholesale disappearance of the small landowner, but undoubtedly, in many counties the old yeoman families gave way to new men, just as the small squires either increased their incomes or disappeared before new standards of living and new fortunes made in trade. This was no new thing in English history, but it was an accelerating process in the eighteenth century. When a class dwindles or disappears, it does not necessarily go under, or even sink in the social scale. Many small freeholders in the later part of the century, when large farmers were making fortunes, sold their land in order to rent large farms, and some of them again bought land. Others, like the Peels, made fortunes in manufacture, and again became landowners, though in King's categories of 'baronets' and 'esquires,' instead of as simple freeholders.

It is not to be doubted that the first half of the eighteenth century was a more prosperous time for working people than the seventeenth century. How far it was a real golden age, and how far it compares favourably with the period between 1750 or 1760 and 1815 is another question and a much more difficult one. That it was a golden age for the squire and still more so for 'the Great' is certain. But there was no revolutionary change between the England of Gregory King and the England of Defoe, more especially where the small farmer and the village labourer were concerned. The poverty of the small farmer persisted. Defoe agrees with Baxter in assuming that the standard of living of the artisan is higher than that of the small farmer. As for food, we can compare for the seventeenth century Baxter's account of the farmer's bacon once a week, his skim milk and skim cheese, with Petty's earlier description of the artisan's menu—bread and cheese, beer, "neck beef and inwards twice a week, stale fish, old pease without butter" —poor fare enough. Defoe, in 1709, some fifty years after Petty, divides the population into seven classes :

1. The Great who live profusely.
2. The rich who live very plentifully.
3. The middle sort who live well.

4. The working trades who labour hard but feel no want.

5. The country people, farmers, etc., who fare indifferently.

5. The poor, that fare hard.

6. The miserable that really pinch and suffer want.[1]

Defoe is writing in praise of English plenty, still there are three grades whose fare is scanty. Above them is the artisan—" Take the fourth sort for a medium . . . suppose a carpenter, a smith, a weaver, or any such workman . . . that is industrious works hard and feels no want, let him live in the country or city. . . . If the gentleman eats more puddings, this man eats more bread, if the rich man drinks more wine, this drinks more ale or strong beer, for it is the support of his labour and strength. If the rich man eats more veal and lamb, fowl and fish, this man eats more beef and bacon, and add to it has a better stomach. As to the milk, if the rich man eats more butter, more cream, more white meats . . . our workman eats more hard cheese and salt butter than all the other put together." This is the artisan, who if

[1] *Review*, June 25, 1709.

industrious and in good work, important qualifications, feels no want. But farmers fare indifferently, while "the poor," that is labouring men as contrasted with artisans, "pinch and suffer want."

It is not to be forgotten that Defoe was disposed to glorify trade at the expense of agriculture. But neither is it to be doubted that throughout the century the lot of the small farmer was hard, and the well-being of the married agricultural labourer depended on the employment of his wife and children. Apart from the crises which from time to time ravaged industrial districts with unemployment, poverty was always greatest in the purely agricultural districts where there was little or no work for women and children.

This possibly golden age of the country-man was a time when there were persistent complaints of hard times from landowners and farmers. People were writing of the disastrous effects of low prices for corn, much as they are writing to-day. The 'corn affair'—over-production and low prices—was a recognised problem about 1736. Rents were in arrears and—so it was said—declining. "Innumerable are the distresses of our farmers, even among those who may be presumed to have good bargains."[1] Bad roads gave farmers a very restricted market and kept prices very low in many districts. Local industries, it was said, were dependent on these low prices, and when roads improved and prices rose, the complaints were of another sort: "The most fruitful parts of England before the roads were mended were natural magazines one half of the year, that is from November to May, the badness of the roads would not allow provisions to be brought from thence. . . . The consequence was, that manufactures were established in those places where labouring people could then afford to work reasonable, as the farmer or dairy man was willing to sell his produce in small quantities. . . . These places are become populous by being manufactories and thereby the inhabitants are become greatly distrest and miserable."[2] That was written in 1772, a year of especially high prices and distress. The good times are always in the past, but the very low prices had meant hard times for farmers and low wages for "manufacturers."

Throughout the century it was assumed that a

[1] W. Allen, *Ways and Means to Raise the Value of Land.* 1736. p. 17.

[2] T. Rooke, Esq. *The Real Causes of the Dearness of Provisions.* . . . Political Register, vi, 71.

man's wages could not be expected to support a family of young children, and long before the Berkshire Justices in 1795 embarked upon their fatal policy at Speenhamland, poor-relief in proportion to the number of children had been customary. A hundred years earlier (in 1697) John Locke drew up a report for the Board of Trade on the problem of poverty and poor-relief. "The children of labouring people," he wrote, "are an ordinary burthen to the parish. . . . A great number of children giving a poor man a title to an allowance from the parish, this allowance is given once a week, or once a month, to the father in money, which he not infrequently spends at the alehouse, whilst his children are left to suffer or perish from the want of necessaries. . . ." He estimated that a labouring man and his wife in health might be able to support two children. He recommended that all children over three should be taught to earn their living at working schools for spinning and knitting, where they should be given bread. "What they can have at home from their parents is seldom more than bread and water, and that very scantily too."

There is nothing in the economic or social history of the earlier eighteenth century to account for any revolutionary change in the position of the small farmers and 'labouring poor' since the days of King, Baxter and Locke. Throughout the century it was accounted a great social service to find employment for women and children since no labouring man could be expected to support a wife and family unaided.

Thirty years after Locke's proposals, Defoe contrasted the lot of the working family where there was employment for women and children and where they had to depend on the man's earnings: The purely agricultural counties he calls the "unemployed counties": "Where the poor are full of work they are never empty of wages; they eat while the others starve, and have a tolerable plenty; while in the unemployed counties it goes hard with them. And whence is all this? Look to the lands, and consequently to the estates of the gentry, the manufacturing counties are calculated for business, the unemployed for pleasure; the first are thronged with villages and great towns,[1] the last with parks and great forests; the first are stored with people, the last with game. . . . The reason of the thing answers for itself; a poor labouring man that goes abroad to his day's work and husbandry, hedging, ditching, threshing, cart-

[1] i.e. townships or villages.

ing, etc., and brings home to his wife his week's wages, suppose at eightpence to twelvepence a day or in some counties less, if he has a wife and three or four children to feed, and get little or nothing for themselves, must fare hard and live poorly; 'tis easy to suppose it must be so.

"But if this man's wife and children can at the same time get employment, if at next door, or at the next village, there lives a clothier or a bay maker or a stuff or drugget weaver: the manufacturer sends the poor woman comb'd wool or carded wool every week to spin, and she gets eightpence or ninepence a day at home; the weaver sends for her two little children, and they work by the loom, winding, filling quills, etc., and the two bigger girls spin at home with their mother, and there earn threepence or fourpence a day each: so that put it together, the family at home gets as much as the father gets abroad and generally more.

"This alters the case, the family feels it . . . and as they grow, they do not run away to be footmen and soldiers—thieves and beggars—or sell themselves to the plantations to avoid the gaol and the gallows; but have a trade at their hands and everyone can get their bread."[1] This is a

[1] *A Plan of the English Commerce*, 1728, 89 ff

characteristically optimistic estimate of the earnings of the wife and children.

It was a universal assumption in the eighteenth century that to provide work for women and children was a great benefit to the nation and an unmixed advantage to "the poor." Defoe on his tour uses the extent of their employment as a criterion of prosperity. And when he discusses (in 1728) the great question of whether trade has grown, or, "as some say, declined," he instances, as convincing proof of advance, the introduction of new industries, notably that of bone lace (or bobbin-made lace), which has the inestimable advantage of employing "those of the most idle, useless and burthensome part of our People (I mean such as were so before) *viz.* the younger women and female children. These were a real charge upon the diligent laborious poor such as the Farmers, the Husbandmen and the Handicrafts of other Trades, and are now made able to provide themselves and ease their parents and parishes of a dead weight which was in many cases insupportable."[1]

[1] It is worth noting that here not only day-labourers but farmers and artisans are classed together as the poor.

High wages and insubordination in towns—low wages, and subordination in the country, was a common theme of early eighteenth-century writers: "Inferior tradesmen, and mechanicks, cottagers, labourers and servants" are thus described by Gonzalez, a self-styled Portuguese, but probably an Englishman, in 1730: "In the City of London and other populous trading towns they generally get a good livelihood—eat and drink well, and on Sundays and holidays appear very well cloathed, and in their own phrase, look upon themselves to be as good as the best, that is, deserve to be treated with respect. Cottagers are not generally so insolent: they have such poor wages and depend so entirely on the gentlemen and farmers that they are ready to pay their masters the respect that is due to them." This writer's account of the state of the poor supports Defoe's picture of 'the unemployed counties.' "The legislature," he says, "has provided abundance of excellent laws for the maintenance of the poor: and manufactures sufficient to employ them all; yet by indolent management few nations are more burdened with them, there not being many countries where the poor are in a worse condition. And one great cause of their increase is, that a poor man, though he has constant work does not earn more than four or five shillings a week (except in London and some other great trading towns), which will barely purchase bread and cheese and clothes for his family; so that if he falls sick or dies his wife and children infallibly come to the parish for relief, who allow them a small pittance, or confine them in a work-house—so as just to keep them from starving, which drives the greater number rather to seek their bread by begging."

This gloomy picture is very far from being universally true.

Still, eightpence, or tenpence, or a shilling a day was the normal agricultural wage, and as Defoe says, " in some counties less." On the other hand harvest work and threshing were paid at a higher rate, but throughout the year there were inevitably off-days through bad weather or want of work. The foreign visitor was almost invariably impressed with the well-being of the English farmer and labourer. In comparison with the Continent standards of life were higher, work was less arduous, cottages and farm-houses were far cleaner and neater. Women worked less hard, farmers and working people were better dressed. Foreigners looked with pleased surprise at the gardens of farm-houses and cottages. This is true of the worst periods of agricultural distress as well as of the so-called golden age before 1760.

Farmers' wives and daughters, remarked a Frenchman in the 'forties, "not only dress but adorn themselves. . . . A young country girl in other countries is a mere peasant, here by the neatness of her dress and the genteelness of her person you would take her for a shepherdess in one of our romances. I know provinces in France where there is no difference between the man and his wife but the petticoat."[1]

The easy-going way in which labouring men frequented the village inn astonished Kalm, a Swedish visitor in 1748. It was not unusual, he says, "to see many sit the whole day at the inn. But the custom of the country that friends and neighbours come together, sit and converse, the abundance of money in this country, the ease with which a man could in every case have his food if only he was somewhat industrious seem to have conduced to this result. . . . It is not to be wondered at, then, if a great many labourers and others, however large the daily wages and profits they can make, can for all that scarcely collect

[1] Le Blanc, *Letters on the English and French Nations*, 1747.

more than what goes from hand to mouth."[1] There was little of the penuriousness of the peasant in England.

What the foreign visitor thought of the Englishman, his freedom, his good food, his easy going comfort, the Englishman on the whole thought of himself. He believed in English liberty and English roast beef, even when he never tasted it. To him wooden shoes were a symbol of French poverty, slavery and popery. Hogarth's *Gate of Calais*, showing the starving Frenchman, the fat monk and the good fare of the Englishman, decorated many humble rooms. Fielding's song, "The Roast Beef of old England," could almost be regarded as the national anthem. In London it was customary for the occupants of the gallery to sing it between the acts of the play.[2]

All this made for contentment, and the greater part of the century was a time of content, though a bad harvest inevitably meant serious food riots. Even the poor law, in spite of the inconceivable hardships which it brought to individuals, and its

[1] Wendeborn, for twenty years a German pastor in London, was much impressed by this characteristic lack of thrift and foresight. See his *View of England towards the Close of the Eighteenth Century*, i., p. 113 ff.

[2] In the frontispiece St. George carries a mighty sirloin on his sword.

disastrous social consequences in certain directions, gave a sense of security and well-being which was new in England. There was a seventeenth-century ballad, now known only by tradition as the name of a tune, called "Hang care, the parish is bound to keep us." In sickness and old age, as well as when he had a number of young children, poor relief was the accepted, inevitable and unresented lot of the labouring man. His settlement he regarded as his birthright or his freehold.

CHAPTER II

DEFOE'S ENGLAND : LONDON AND THE COUNTRY.

TO counteract our bad habit of reading history backwards and looking at the past only from the standpoint of the present, we must read contemporary books, for their point of view as well as for their information. Far the best authority for early eighteenth-century England is Defoe. His famous *Tour through the whole Island of Great Britain* shows us the country as it appeared to a skilled observer with a marvellous eye for significant detail, who was also a man of business as well as a consummate journalist. This book at once corrects our instinct to regard the past as old-fashioned or worse still, quaint, and to forget that each age, for those who live in it, is in the forefront of modernity. To us, the England of the seventeen-twenties is a static, agricultural country, with considerable trade perhaps, but with rudimentary industries. To Defoe, it is a country of trade and manufacture and of rapid economic development. Things are in a state of flux. "New discoveries in metals, mines and minerals," he writes, "new undertakings in trade, engines, manufactures, in a nation pushing and improving as we are; these things open new scenes every day, and make England especially shew a new and differing face in many places, on every occasion of surveying it."

There is one thing which stands out clearly—the enormous importance of London. London was then far more important, commercially, industrially and socially, in relation to the rest of the country than it has ever been since. London was the only great city in England where town life was sharply cut off from country life. The only place it could be compared with was Paris, and people were fond of discussing which was the larger and which the more wicked. At the end of the seventeenth century London had more than a tenth of the population of England and Wales. Out of a total of about 5½ millions London's share is estimated at 674,000 odd. And enormous as a town population of over half a million then was, the place impressed people as so colossal that there were sober calculators who made out that it had at least a million inhabitants. Defoe even accepts an estimate of a million and a half: "Suppose the City of London (of course he means greater London, not the square mile of the City) to contain fifteen hundred thousand people as they tell us it does," he writes. This by the way should serve as a warning to accept his figures with reservation. When, for instance, he boasts of the number employed in manufactures and of the vast fortunes made in trade, it is well to remember his disposition to glorify everything connected with British trade.

London was then the chief centre of trade in the country. By far the greater part of the imports and exports came in and went out of the port of London. London was also the centre and clearing house of inland trade, since heavy goods were transported chiefly by coasting vessels and up navigable rivers, the Thames of course being the most important. Country producers depended to a great extent on London merchants and warehousemen for the sale and export of their goods, and many kinds of textiles were sent to London for finishing processes such as pressing, dyeing and printing. The great industries connected with shipping and export naturally flourished there. These were highly capitalised businesses on modern lines, such as breweries, distilleries, sugar refineries. London-made goods then as now had a reputation for special excellence ; her cutlery was reputed better than that of Sheffield. London clocks and watches by the end of the seventeenth century were renowned as the best in the world.

London was in many ways surprisingly modern. There was a penny post with a number of deliveries a day. It had recently become a branch of the General Post Office after having been a private venture. Defoe does it full justice : "Nothing can be more exact," he writes, "and 'tis with the utmost safety and dispatch that letters are delivered at the remotest corners of the town, almost as soon as they could be sent by a messenger, and that from four, five, six to eight times a day, according as the distance of the place makes it practicable ; and you may send a letter from Ratcliffe in the East to the farthest part of Westminster for a penny, and that several times in the same day. Nor are you tied to a single piece of paper, as at the General Post Office, but any pacquet under a pound weight goes at the same price." He justly concluded that it was "a manifest testimony to the greatness of this city and to the great extent of business and commerce in it, that this penny contrivance should raise so many thousand pounds in a year, and employ so many poor people in the diligence of it as this Office employs."

There was another recent development in London which Defoe regarded with suspicion and distrust, almost with horror. This was the gaily decorated shop with glass windows in which pretty trifles were displayed. The shops of an earlier date had been either warehouses piled up with the staple English manufactures—the cloths and kersies, for instance, of the drapers—or little more than stalls. The milliners and pamphlet sellers in particular kept stalls in Westminster Hall. The goldsmiths alone of the more dignified trades appear to have laid out goods for display and even then only their less valuable goods. The increase of shops selling new-fangled luxuries appeared to him signs of degeneracy and impending ruin.

Many of the pernicious luxury-shops were the direct result of the fashion for drinking tea, coffee and chocolate: "Coffee, tea, and Chocolate," Defoe complained in 1713, " . . . are now become capital branches of this nation's commerce. Let any man who remembers the glorious state of our town about forty years ago view but the streets of this opulent city." This appeal to a golden age in the past is as fallacious as such appeals are wont to be, and it will be instructive to test it, instead of taking it for granted. Forty years back would take us to 1673, when complaints of bad trade were rife, and the City (and not least the shopkeepers of St. Paul's Church Yard with whom Defoe is more particularly concerned) was still suffering from the effects of the Great Fire. And there was the recent catastrophe of 1672, known as the Closing of the Exchequer, when Charles was unable to repay the Goldsmiths' or bankers' loan, and reduced the rate of interest from 12% to 6%. Though this was neither so calamitous nor so reprehensible as is often supposed, it ruined a number of bankers and brought disaster to many of their customers. To return to 1713:

"First let him reckon up," Defoe goes on, "all the houses that are now to let and are actually shut up, and then let him set aside all the pastry cooks, coffee houses, perriwig makers, cane chair men, looking glass shops, tinkers, china and earthenware men, brandy shops and the like, whose places of trade used to be found only in back streets, lanes and allies and are fittest for such places. . . . We find the most noble shops in the city taken up with the valuable utensils of the tea table. . . . Two thousand pounds reckoned a small stock in copper pots and lacker'd kettles, and the very fitting up one of these brazen people's shops (he means the braziers who sold the goods) with fine sashes (that is, sash-windows), etc., costs above £500 sterling, which is more by half than the best draper's or mercer's shop in London requires. This certainly shows the increase of our trade," he says ironically, " brass locks for our doors, chambers and parlours, brass knockers for our doors and the like, add to the lustre of our shops . . . and the same sash works and shop windows, only finer and larger, are now used to range your brass and copper, that the goldsmiths had always to set out their less valuable silver and gold plate. . . . How do pastry cooks and perriwig makers, brandy shops and toy shops succeed linen drapers, mercers, upholsterers and the like, a hundred pound rent for a house to sell jellies and apple pies, two hundred pound to set up a brandy shop and afterwards not a hundred pound stock to put into it. . . . View the famous Churchyard of St. Pauls ! . . . What takes up the whole row there and supplies the place of eighteen or nineteen topping drapers ? Who can but observe it! Cane chair makers, guilders of leather, looking glass shops—and pedlars or toy shops. . . ."[1] A toy shop did not then cater for the wants of children, but sold trinkets and such things as buckles and snuff boxes.

This is a complaint against a tendency which was only beginning when Defoe wrote: Expenditure on the setting out of goods so as to attract customers. This form of advertisement was new when he wrote—he thought the prudent trader should sink his capital in the wares which he sold. His indignation against this new-fangled custom is combined with dislike of the new luxury trades which were encroaching on the old staple trades of the drapers and mercers: "It is a modern custom and wholly unknown to our ancestors, who yet understood trade in proportion to the trade they carried on, as well as we do, to have tradesmen lay out two-thirds of their fortune in fitting up their shops.

"By fitting up, I do not mean furnishing their shops with wares and goods to sell; for in that they came up to us in every particular, and perhaps went beyond us too; but in painting and gilding, fine shelves, shutters, boxes, glass doors, sashes and

[1] *Review*, 1713.

the like, in which they tell us now, 'tis a small matter to lay out two or three hundred pounds, nay, five hundred pounds, to fit up a pastry cook's, or a toy shop. . . .

"It will hardly be believed in ages to come, when our posterity shall be grown wiser by our loss, and, as I may truly say, at our expense, that a pastry cook's shop, which twenty pounds would effectively furnish at a time, with all needful things for sale, yet that fitting up one of these shops should cost upwards of 300*l*, *Anno Domini*, 1710, let the year be recorded." As this throws light on a rather obscure subject—the evolution of the shop—it is worth quoting at some length. He goes on to describe the windows and the tiled walls of the pastry cook's shop which had roused his spleen, its sash-windows with panes of plate-glass twelve inches by sixteen—a great innovation on the old lattice windows with diamonds or circles of leaded glass. (In another mood he is able to exult over the new industry of making "looking-glass plates.") The walls of the front and back shop are lined with galley tiles, and in both there are large pier looking-glasses. They are beautifully lighted, each with a large branch candlestick or chandelier, as well as great glass lanterns, three large and eight small, and twenty-five sconces against the walls. In the back room is a large pair of silver standing candlesticks. There are silver salvers to set out the wares and "twelve large high stands or rings, whereof, three silver, to place small dishes for tarts, jellys, etc., at a feast." The painting of the ceiling, the gilding of the lanterns and the windows and the "carved work" cost no less than £55. All this with china and "other things to make a shew" cost more than £300. "So that in short, here was a trade, which might have been carried on for about 30 or 40*l* stock, required 300*l* expence to fit up the shop and make a shew to invite customers." Such an extravagant outlay, he thinks, "will hardly be believed in ages to come, when our posterity shall be grown wiser at our expense."[1]

Defoe's outburst is an excellent illustration of a characteristic of the trade and industry of the times; then capital was sunk in stock, and used for wages, and to a large extent for giving credit to customers, but very little was used for buildings and what are now called overhead expenses. But it is unlike Defoe to look so bleakly on new developments in trade; he had a remarkably forward-

[1] *The Compleat English Tradesman,* 1726, i, 312–15.

seeing eye and here he is looking backwards. But he has seized upon an early stage of a process which has gone immeasurably farther since his day, and whose end is not in sight: the progressive encroachment of luxury trades on old and basic industries, and the supplying of new wants and amenities in addition to the necessities of life. The braziers' shops and 'toy shops,' the pastry cooks' which made Defoe splenetic are the forerunners of vast industries based on the creation of new desires: "the motor-cycle, the motor-car, the gramophone, the radio, artificial silk, the cinema, the popular press, books, travel facilities, greyhound races. . . ."[1]

London, with its noisy crowded streets, lighted shop windows, its post office, and its embryo stock exchange at Jonathan's coffee house, and the speculations of the bulls and bears of Change Alley and the astonishing brilliance and luxury of its shops, its legendary and fascinating wickedness, seemed to belong to a different world and a different age from the country village and the country town. The lure of London as a place where fortunes were to be made, where life was

[1] Prof. T. E. Gregory, *Rationalization and Technological Unemployment*. 'Econ. Journal.' Dec., 1930.

altogether on an easier, more luxurious scale was tremendous. And country people, when they came to town were so conspicuously different from Londoners, and gazed about with such open-mouthed wonder that they were an easy prey to sharpers and harpies of both sexes.

In appearance the country by comparison had changed strangely little since the Middle Ages. Although wastes, commons, forests and marshes had been steadily diminishing by the encroachment of cultivation and the ravages of wood cutters, in the early eighteenth century large tracts of country were still in a primeval state of wildness.

Much of the land was still in the great open fields of the medieval village, where each cultivator's land was dispersed in many scattered strips. Roads, though improving, were still very bad, and in winter sometimes impassable for waggons. Nevertheless the country had long outgrown the stage where country districts were self-supporting and the local farmers, smiths, carpenters and weavers supplied the needs of its inhabitants. Agriculture had been profoundly affected by the need for providing food for London. The London demand had fostered stock and dairy farming; and the business of transport and marketing was

highly organized. For instance, Cheshire was supplying London with more than half of the enormous quantities of cheese consumed there; the London cheesemongers had a line of vessels plying between Chester and the capital, and they also employed waggons. Then as now turkeys came from Norfolk, but the poor birds made the journey on foot. And though some counties were, as Defoe says, merely agricultural, these were few. England was covered with dispersed and highly specialized industries carried on largely in country districts with their headquarters in neighbouring towns.

The great woollen industry was chiefly centred in three districts: the south-west, long famous for its fine cloths; the eastern counties round Norwich which specialized in worsteds, and the West Riding where cheaper cloths were made. Metal industries and hardware covered the districts round Birmingham, Sheffield and Walsall; the hosiery trades had their headquarters at Derby, Nottingham and Leicester. Coal was being produced on a large scale in Northumberland and Durham, and Cumberland, on a small scale at Kingswood and in the Forest of Dean; the pits of Warwickshire, Lancashire and Yorkshire came between the two extremes.

A large fleet of colliers traded between London and the Tyne.[1]

It is surprising to find how many places by the seventeen-twenties were already noted for the industries which are still among their staple products. Defoe describes with great gusto the complicated organization by which these scattered industries supplied the home and foreign trade. Far from complaining of the extortion of the middleman, he glories in the fact that, for instance, a piece of cloth would go through ten tradesmen's hands before it came to the last consumer. This, he says, "is that which makes our trade be so immensely great." He explains the nature of the home trade by concrete examples. The materials to clothe a small farmer (whom he calls "the poorest countryman"), or a gentleman's servant in or out of livery, will come from almost every one of the "manufacturing counties" (He is using the word manufacture, as it was then often used, to mean pre-eminently the textile industries). His fascinating recital is not only a survey of the distribution of industries, but gives a vivid picture of the dress and household goods of humble people

[1] T. S. Ashton and J. Sykes, *The Coal Industry of the Eighteenth Century*, 1929.

two centuries ago. The cloth for the man's coat comes from Yorkshire; it is lined with shalloon (a thin woollen stuff) from Berkshire. The waistcoat is of calamanco (woollen or worsted material usually with a glossy surface) from Norwich. The breeches are " of a strong drugget from the Devizes, Wilts." (Leather breeches were also much worn by working people.) His yarn stockings are from Westmoreland. His hat is a felt from Leicester. His leather gloves come from Somerset, his shoes from Northampton. His buttons, if of material, come from Macclesfield, if of metal from Birmingham. His garters come from Manchester, and his shirt of British linen from Lancashire or Scotland. Thus one suit of clothes of the most ordinary kind, Defoe points out, employs almost every manufacturing county in England.

In the furnishing of a house the same holds good, and Defoe next describes the clothes and household goods of a " middling tradesman " and his wife in a country town. He takes as his example a grocer, at such a place as Horsham, since it is in the middle of Sussex, a county where, he says, very few if any ' manufactures ' are carried on. The man's clothes would be much the same as those already described, but since his coat is of rather finer cloth it comes from Wiltshire instead of Yorkshire; and as his stockings may be of worsted in place of yarn they come from Nottingham instead of Westmoreland. His wife's dress is next described, and she "being a good honest tradesman's daughter, is not dressed over-fine, yet she must have something decent, being new married, too, and especially as times go, when the burghers' wives of Horsham or any other town go as fine as they do in other places; allow her then to have a silk gown, and all the necessaries belonging to a middling tolerable appearance, yet you shall find all the nation more or less concern'd in cloathing this country grocer's wife, and furnishing her house, and yet nothing extraordinary." Her gown is a plain English mantua silk made in Spitalfields, her petticoat the same. (These are both part of her dress which, in modern jargon, was a two-piece.) Her binding is a piece of chequered stuff, made at Bristol or Norwich. This probably corresponds to the stomacher of an earlier period which survived in the stays (also called bodice or jumps) worn by working women as an outside garment till the end of the eighteenth century. Her under-petticoat is "a piece of black calamanco made at Norwich, quilted at home, if she be a good house-wife; but the quilting of cotton from

Manchester or cotton-wool from abroad." Her inner petticoats are of flannel and swanskin from Salisbury and Wales. Her stockings are "from Tewkesbury if ordinary; from Leicester if woven." Her lace is from Stony-stratford, her edgings from Great Marlow. Her muslin is "from foreign trade; as likewise her linen, being something finer than the man's, may perhaps be a Guilick-Holland." Her wrapper or morning-gown is a piece of Irish linen with a pattern printed in London. Her lambskin gloves come from Berwick and Northumberland or Scotland. "Her ribbands being but very few [are] from Coventry or London." Her riding hood is made of worsted-camlet from Norwich.

Defoe then catalogues the furniture of their house: "It is scarce credible, to how many counties of England, and how remote, the furniture of but a mean house must send them; and how many people are everywhere employed about it, nay, the meaner the furniture, the more people and places employ'd. . . . " (The furnishings of a rich man's house would come chiefly from London where the upholsterers, cabinet makers, looking-glass makers, braziers, and grate and stove smiths and many other shopkeeping craftsmen and manufacturers made goods of the highest grade.)

" The Hangings, suppose them to be of ordinary linsey woolsey, are made at Kiddermister, dy'd in the country and painted or water'd at London. The chairs, if of cane, are made at London ; if the ordinary matted chairs, perhaps in the place where they live." Tables, chests of drawers, etc., are made in London, as also looking-glasses.

The bedding includes the curtains which might be of serge from Taunton or Exeter, or of camlet from Norwich, or of linsey woolsey like the hangings. The ticking for mattresses and pillows like the feathers is " from the West-country, Somerset or Dorset." The blankets are from Witney, the rugs from Westmoreland or Yorkshire. The sheets, if of good linen, are from Ireland. " The kitchen utensils and chimney furniture, almost all of brass, and iron [are] from Birmingham and Sheffield."

It is the supreme achievement of " inland trade," in Defoe's opinion, that all these household goods and materials for clothes and furnishings are provided by the local shopkeeper, who does not deal with the first producer but with wholesale dealers in London, who not only furnish the country shopkeepers, but give them large credit. Between the producer and the wholesale dealer there are agents—factors or middlemen ; this makes "a general circulation of trade" and "every manufacture is sold and remov'd five or six times before it comes to the last consumer." Defoe had himself been an agent or factor supplying goods to the London hosiers, so that he speaks from personal knowledge.

It would be clearly a mistake to take this literally as the way in which the people of country towns did in general furnish their houses. Defoe takes no account of the local smith and carpenter; he is not interested in their productions, but is concerned to show the general achievements of trade. This is a lesson in industrial geography, rather than an accurate individual picture. It is much as if a modern writer were to assert that country people were all supplied with food and furniture by long-distance motor vans from large stores in big towns. Some are, and almost all could be, so supplied, yet the local producer and the village shop survive. But as a survey of industry and a picture of the clothes and household goods of humble people Defoe's catalogue is an invaluable picture. It is clear that the age of comfort has begun. He also shows, though without stressing it, the much-deplored weak spot in English trade: muslins, lawns and fine linens cannot be supplied from home industries, and even the better sort of linen sheets come from Ireland. The superiority of French cambrics and Holland lawns was a perennial source of humiliation, and East India muslins were eagerly imported in the hope that they would compete at home and abroad with French and Dutch goods. But the great desire was for a home manufacture which would supplant them, and create a new source of employment for women and children. When the inventions of Arkwright and Crompton led to the production and perfection of British muslins the conscious aims of a century were achieved.[1]

Another caution is necessary before we accept Defoe's picture. His country grocer lived in Sussex, and the southern counties and the counties round London differed widely from the more backward districts in Wales and the North. The North of England was then thinly populated and industrially backward except for Tyneside with its coal, the West Riding with its cloth industry and the country round the very rapidly growing port of Liverpool. Social history is local history. The North of England is even now in many ways a different world from the South; for instance, the domestic

[1] See below, p. 149.

baking of bread is common in very humble homes in Yorkshire, in the South it is a luxury of the well-to-do. The possibility of household weaving is ignored by Defoe, and not even stockings and garters are knitted at home. Kalm, the Swede (in 1748), was amazed to find bread-making, weaving and spinning almost unknown occupations in the farmhouses of Hertfordshire and Essex. But at the end of the century in the North the clothes worn by farmers and even labourers were made of home-spun thread or yarn woven by a local weaver : "Almost every article of dress worn by farmers, mechanics and labourers is manufactured at home, shoes and hats excepted ; that is, the linen thread is spun from the lint, so that almost every family has its web of linen cloth annually, and often one of woollen also, which is either dyed for coats or made into flannel, etc. . . . Although broad cloth, purchased in the shops, begins now to be worn by opulent farmers and others on Sundays, yet there are many respectable persons at this day who never wore a bought pair of stockings, coat nor waistcoat in their lives : and within these twenty years, a coat bought at a shop was considered a mark of extravagance and pride, if a man was not a man of independent fortune." But the poorest labourers could not afford to buy the necessary wool or yarn and clothes could be bought in the shops which were much cheaper than those made at home, though they were inferior both in warmth and durability.

Defoe was writing seventy years before the state of things here described in Sir William Eden's *State of the Poor*, and in the meantime manufactured and shop-provided goods had been continuing their encroachment on the home-producer.

The manufactures described by Defoe were for the most part organized on what is called the domestic system. This is an unsatisfactory term because it covers such different variations as the small producer who sells his wares to a merchant or middleman and the workman who is provided with materials which he works up at home for piece-rate wages, often performing only one of a number of processes which go to make the finished article. Such were the combers, carders, spinners in many branches of the wool trade. This system flourished in England from the sixteenth to the eighteenth century and still survives. But from the social point of view, the most significant change produced by the industrial revolution has been the coming of the modern factory system, where the capitalist employer supplies buildings, machinery and material and controls every stage of production. The power-loom in the factory has superseded the hand-loom in the cottage. Even in Defoe's day some industries were already in the modern stage, but what we are concerned with now is the domestic system. The variations in this system, in different places, different trades and in different branches of the same trade, are so great that it is difficult to generalize about it—at all events it must be the subject of a separate chapter.

CHAPTER III

THE PRELUDE TO THE MACHINE AGE

THE domestic system has been idealized, much as the medieval gild has been idealized, partly because it has been misunderstood, partly by comparison with the evils of the early factories and indeed of machine production in general. It had the great advantage that in general the workers lived in the country—in general, but by no means always—there were looms in Manchester, in the garrets of Norwich, in the tenement houses of London, not to speak of smaller towns. But on the whole the aim of the capitalist employer was to seek labour where it was cheapest and this was in the country districts.

'Capitalist employer' may sound out of place in an account of the domestic system. The picture evoked by the thought of a typical eighteenth-century workman is of a cottage interior after the

Wm. Hincks, Del. et Sculp. *Pubd. 1791*

LINEN MAKING IN COUNTY DOWN

Representing Spinning, Reeling with the Clock Reel, and Boiling the Yarn

[*face p.* 54

manner of Morland ; a weaver sits at his loom, his wife at her spinning wheel, children play on the floor. It is vaguely supposed that the man is a small farmer, working alternately at the loom and on the land, and disposing of his cloth in the market. There were farmer-weavers of this sort in backward parts of the country—in the north and in Wales. They survived into the nineteenth century among the Irish linen weavers, and they still exist among the crofters of the Scottish Highlands. But even in the eighteenth century they were an exception in England. For the most part farmers were farmers and weavers were weavers. In harvest time spinners and carders and sometimes weavers left their usual work for the better earnings of the harvest field. Nailors did the same to the obstruction of overseas trade. A quaker merchant during the Seven Years War explains to a customer in America the delay in dispatching consignments of nails : " Our nailors are so much out in harvest time."[1]

The idealization of the domestic weaver which finds its way into text-books is largely based on a famous description by Defoe of the woollen industry round Halifax. It is a delightful

[1] *English Historical Review*, xxxi, 143.

description, and bits of it have been much quoted. I will quote from it now, but it should be read at length and in its own context. Defoe, travelling from the south, found the district very populous : " the nearer we came to Halifax, we found the houses thicker, and the villages greater in every bottom; and not only so, but the sides of the hills, which were very steep every way, were spread with houses, and that very thick ; for the land being divided into small enclosures, that is to say, from two acres to six or seven acres each, seldom more ; every three or four pieces of land had a house belonging to it.

" Then it was I began to perceive the reason and nature of the thing, and found that this division of the land into small pieces, and scattering of the dwellings was occasioned by, and done for the convenience of the business which the people were generally employed in, and . . . though we saw no people stirring without doors, yet they were all full within . . . not a beggar, not an idle person to be seen, except here and there an almshouse, where people antient, decrepid—and past labour might perhaps be found, for it is observable—that the people here, however laborious, generally live to a great age, a certain testimony of the goodness and wholesomeness of the country . . . nor is the health of the people lessen'd but help'd and establish'd by their being constantly employ'd, and, as we call it their working hard. . . . Such has been the bounty of nature to this otherwise frightful country, that two things essential to the business . . . are found here . . . and I believe the like is not to be seen so contrived in any part of the world: I mean coals and running water upon the tops of the highest hills: This seems to have been directed by the wise hand of Providence for the very purpose which is now served by it, namely the manufactures, which otherwise could not be carried on; neither indeed could one fifth part of the inhabitants be supported without them, for the land could not maintain them. . . . We could see that almost at every house there was a tenter, and almost on every tenter a piece of cloth, or kersie or shalloon, for they are the three articles of that country's labour. . . .

" . . . at every considerable house was a manufactory or work-house and as they could not do their business without water, the little streams were so parted and guided by gutters and pipes, and by turning and dividing the streams, that none of those houses were without a river, if I may call it so, running into and through their work-houses . . .

"Then as every clothier must keep a horse, perhaps two, to fetch and carry for the use of his manufacture (*viz.*) to fetch home his wool and his provisions from the market, to carry his yarn to the spinners, his manufacture to the fulling mill, and when finished, to the market to be sold, and the like; so every manufacturer generally keeps a cow or two, or more, for his family, and this employs the two or three or four pieces of enclosed land about his house, for they scarce sow corn enough for their cocks and hens. . . ."

Among the hills are not only streams but coal pits, which are easy to work: "having thus fire and water at every dwelling, there is no reason to enquire why they dwell thus dispersed among the highest hills, the convenience of the manufacturers requiring it. Among the manufacturers' houses are likewise scattered an infinite number of cottages, in which dwell the workmen that are employed, the women and children of whom are always busy, carding, spinning, etc., even from the youngest to the antient; hardly any thing above four years old, but its hands are sufficient to itself.

" That is the reason also why we saw so few people without doors ; but if we knock'd at the door of any of the master manufacturers, we presently saw a house full of lusty fellows, some at the dye-fat, some dressing the cloths, some in the loom, some one thing, some another all hard at work and full employment upon the manufacture, and all seeming to have sufficient business."

Things jump to the eye of the reader of this passage which have yet been ignored or misinterpreted. Defoe describes it in detail because it is strange to him and will be strange to his readers. As he says of inhabitants of the country north of the Trent, " their customs and genius differing so much from others, will add to our entertainment." The little enclosures of pasture, the scattered houses, are in marked contrast with the open arable strips and the farms concentrated in the village street which were common in most counties in the South and Midlands. He is struck by the absence of unemployed people and beggars, " all seeming to have sufficient business." The manufacture is an absolute necessity, for the land alone could not support the population : there is no arable farming, and " as to beef and mutton they feed little or none." Moreover, the manufacture is made possible by the exceptional character of the country, with its coals and water. The large houses are little manufactories, owned by the master-clothiers, the men they employ live in "an infinite number of cottages." These are without land, a fact implicit in Defoe's description and expressly stated by Arthur Young, when he visited the district in 1795: "Their land is generally at 40s. an acre, it is only the master-clothier that has it; the loom-men in the cottages have none . . . but are assisted in milk. . . . "[1] This small but prosperous employer has been compared, most unfairly, with the factory worker, or with the hand-loom weaver who has fallen on evil days.

Then, this Halifax wool industry is not, properly speaking, an example of domestic industry.[2] The men work on their employer's premises. It can be regarded either as a belated example of guild methods—though outside the limits of towns and

[1] *Annals of Agriculture*, xxvii, 310–11. This would probably not exclude a garden or potato-patch. Professor Heaton says few cottages in the West Riding were without a piece of land.—*Yorkshire Woollen and Worsted Industries.*

[2] Though it was so styled in the *Report on the State of the Woollen Manufactures*, 1806.

corporations—in which the master works himself surrounded by his journeymen and apprentices; or as an early example of factory industry, on a small scale and without power (though water power was used for fulling-mills). The great merit of the system Defoe describes is that little capital was needed to set up as a master, and there was no wide gulf between master and man. But this was exceptional. It applied only to a strictly limited part of the West Riding: the cloth trade was confined to a pentagon whose five points were Wakefield, Huddersfield, Halifax, Bradford and Leeds. And even in this district by no means all the masters were small men. The worsted trade which centred in Bradford as the cloth trade did in Leeds scarcely existed before the second decade of the eighteenth century, and from the beginning was in the hands of men employing more capital and labour.

The agriculture, too, of these master weavers was rudimentary (to put it mildly) and entirely secondary to their industrial interests. This was the district that Cobbett called (in 1832) "as to *agriculture*, certainly the poorest country that I have ever set eyes on, except that miserable *Nova Scotia*. . . ."

It is characteristic of Defoe's attitude to trade and agriculture that he maintains that it is the industrial part of the county which supports the agricultural part, by consuming the food the other produces: "since they sow hardly enough corn to feed their poultry"; "and as to beef and mutton, they feed little or none . . . they must then necessarily have their provisions from other parts of the country. . . . Their corn comes up in great quantities out of Lincoln, Nottingham and the East Riding, their black cattle and horses from the North Riding, their sheep and mutton from the adjacent counties every way, their butter from the East and North Riding, their cheese out of Cheshire and Warwickshire, more black cattle also from Lancashire. And here the breeders and feeders, the farmers and country people find money flowing in plenty from the manufacturers and commerce."

This small Yorkshire cloth district with its thriving trade was so exceptional in eighteeth-century England that it fascinated contemporaries; the small masters, the supposed absence of labour disputes in contrast with conditions elsewhere were the aspects which were selected for admiration, just as they have been in modern times. Dean

Tucker, who knew the South West thoroughly and Yorkshire much less well, wrote of the small farmers and freeholders who spun and wove yarn, and sold it on commission in Leeds market. Their journeymen, he wrote in 1757, "if they have any, being so little removed from the degree and condition of their masters, and so likely to set up for themselves by the industry and frugality of a few years, have no conception that they are embarked in an interest opposite to that of their masters, or that they are called upon to enter clubs and combinations against them. Thus it is that the goods are well made and exceedingly cheap and that a riot or a mob is a thing hardly known among them. Whereas in Gloucestershire, Wiltshire and Somersetshire the manufacture is carried on by a quite different process, and the effects are accordingly; *viz.*, one person with a great stock and large credit, buys the wool, pays for the spinning, weaving, milling, dyeing, shearing, dressing, etc. That is, he is the master of the whole manufacture from first to last and perhaps employs a thousand persons under him. This is the clothier whom all the rest are to look upon as their paymaster. But will they not also sometimes look upon him as their tyrant? And as great numbers of them work together in the same shop, will they not have it the more in their power to vitiate and corrupt each other, to cabal and associate against their masters and to break out into mobs and riots upon every little occasion? The event hath fully shewed and is now shewing that these conjectures are too frequently supported by facts. . . . The master . . . however well disposed himself is continually tempted by his situation to be proud and overbearing, to consider his people as the scum of the earth, whom he has a right to squeeze whenever he can; because they ought to be kept low and not to rise up in competition with their superiors. The journeymen on the contrary are equally tempted by their situation to envy the high station and superior fortunes of their masters; and to envy them the more in proportion as they find themselves deprived of the hopes of advancing themselves to the same degree by any stretch of industry or superior skill. Hence their self-love takes a wrong turn, destructive to themselves and others. They think it no crime to get as much wages and do as little for it as they possibly can, to lie and cheat and do any other bad thing, provided it is only against their master and their common enemy, with whom no faith is to be kept. The motives to industry, frugality, and sobriety are all subverted by this one consideration, *viz.*, that they shall always be chained to the same oar and never be but journeymen. Therefore their only happiness is to get drunk and to make life pass away with as little thought as possible. This being the case, is it to be wondered at that the trade in Yorkshire should flourish, or the trade in Somersetshire, Wiltshire, and Gloucestershire be found declining every day ? "[1]

This is the voice of an economist with a special knowledge of the clothing district of the South West. The Yorkshire cloth trade was by no means so immune from labour troubles as he supposed, but they were of course much less than in districts where the industry was more highly capitalized and where the journeymen felt themselves " always chained to the same oar." Defoe goes to the root of the matter when he sums up the great advantage to England of the cloth industry of the South West : " It maintains so many poor families and makes so many rich ones."[2] The gulf between the wealthy clothier who lived like a country gentleman and the isolated and very poor weavers and spinners to

[1] J. Tucker, *Instructions for Travellers*, 1757, 23–24.

[2] Cp. *Letters from a Moor*, 1736, p. 168. "And I think it . . . very proper to observe to you, what advantage these working people [in Norwich] are in general to the English nation ; they just get enough to keep life and soul together, as their phrase is, while great numbers of people who have some fortune, but more cunning, get estates out of their industry."

whom his agents gave out work was at least as wide as that between the modern factory owner and his workpeople—who are certainly not regarded (as in Tucker's day) as "the scum of the earth." And the gulf was then widened by bitter disputes about the embezzling of materials and deceitful workmanship on one side and payment in truck and unfair deductions for bad work on the other.

A ballad, probably of the late seventeenth century, voices the attitude of the men to the masters: *The Clothier's Delight, or, the Rich Man's Joy, and the Poor Man's Sorrow, wherein is exprest the Craftiness and Subtility of many Clothiers in England by beating down their Workmen's Wages* was sung to the popular tune of *Packington's Pound.*[1] It is the clothier who speaks:

> Of all sorts of callings that in England be
> There is none that liveth so gallant as we;
> Our trading maintains us as brave as a knight.
> We live at our pleasure and take our delight:
> We heapeth up riches and treasure great store
> Which we get by griping and grinding the poor.
> And this is the way for to fill up our purse
> Although we do get with it many a curse.

[1] This is given in full by J Burnley, *History of Wool and Woolcombing*, 1883, pp. 161-3.

As usual there is the legend of better times in the past:

In former ages we us'd to give
So that our work-folks like farmers did live;
But the times are altered, we will make them know
All we can for to bring them all under our bow,
We will make them to work hard for sixpence a day
Though a shilling they deserve if they had their just pay.
And this, etc.

We'll make the poor weavers work at a low rate,
We'll find fault where there is none, and so we will bate;
If trading goes dead, we will presently[1] show it,
But if it grows good, they shall never know it;
We'll tell them that cloth beyond sea will not go,
We care not whether we keep clothing or no.
And this, etc.

The spinners are made "to spin three pounds for two," but if their work is light weight by so much as an ounce,

"Then for to bate threepence we will not be slack."

Payment in truck is the clothier's next trick:

But if it holds weight, then their wages they crave,
We have got no money, and what's that you'd have?
We have bread and bacon and butter that's good,
With oatmeal and salt that's wholesome for food;
We have soap and candles whereby we have light,
That you may work by them so long as you have sight.
And this, etc.

[1] *i.e.* Instantly.

The masters extort twopence from the alewife for every shilling the men spend in the alehouse:

By such cunning ways we our treasure do get,
For it is all fish that doth come to our net.
    And this, etc.

The ballad ends:

Then hey for the clothing trade it goes on brave,
We scorn for to moyl and toyl nor yet to slave,
Our workmen do work hard, but we live at ease;
We go when we will, and come when we please,
We hoard up our bags of silver and gold,
But conscience and charity with us are cold.
    By poor people's labour we fill up our purse
    Although we do get with it many a curse.

The ballad touches on one of the great evils of the domestic system, the way in which the burden of bad trade was thrown on the workpeople, "If trading goes dead we will presently show it." Since the employer had not sunk his money in machines and buildings which eat their heads off if they are not kept going, it was fatally easy for him to stop giving out work and throw the whole burden of unemployment on his out-workers with their tools and workshops, whether these were the looms of the weavers or the anvils and smithies of the nailers and file-makers in the Midlands.

In the hosiery trades of Leicester and Nottingham it was customary (but not universal) for the workers to hire stocking frames from the employers. This made things worse, for frame rent was charged whether work was given out or not.

On the other hand this probably increased the resiliency of trade: the employer, when demand revived, was not burdened with heavy debts incurred in bad times, and so, perhaps, the sum-total of unemployment may have been less than when industry is more highly capitalized. But at all events its brunt was borne by the work-people. To quote Defoe, the poor spinners and workfolk are dismissed to starve.[1]

We know, or think we know, that one of the worst consequences of the Industrial Revolution in the early nineteenth century was that mass production and the growing dependence of producers on distant markets made trade more fluctuating—speculative trading increased, and commercial crises became frequent. It is sometimes assumed that before this, employment was stable and regular. Nothing can be further from the truth, though of course, then as now, there were people in favourable positions. The small minority

[1] See below, p. 72.

who combined industry with agriculture were lucky. Industry was organized for foreign trade long before the days of machine production. In the eighteenth century in spite of the general growth of trade, there were some acute trade crises and over-production and over-speculation reacted disastrously on employers and employed. During the century England repeatedly suffered the dislocating change from peace to war and war to peace; parliamentary committees reported on unemployment and starving workers in different trades.

There is a belief that irregularity of employment is a modern disease. It has even been asserted that trade crises did not arise before the end of the eighteenth century. This is far indeed from the truth. The nature of the trade cycle, and of crises of unemployment, was of course even less understood then than now, but that there was an alternating rhythm of boom and slump, much affected by political causes (and mitigated by the progressive growth of trade), is fairly clear. Defoe describes it vividly: First comes the boom, an unusual demand for goods "upon some sudden accident in trade causes large orders from the factors to the manufacturers, the price of goods always rises according to the demand: the country manufacturer looks out sharp, hires more looms, gets more spinners, gives more wages, and animated by the advanc'd price is not content to answer his new orders only . . . [but] runs on to an extremity in quantity as far or perhaps further than his Stock will allow; and in a word, gluts the market with the goods. . . . Trade returns to its usual channel, but the Manufacturer in the country . . . having not stopt his hand as his orders stopt falls into the Mine; his goods lye on hand, the Poor which he call'd from the Plow and the Dary to spin and weave are cast off again, and not finding their way presently back to their old Drudgery, lye and starve for want of trade, and then they cry out that Trade is decay'd, the Manufactures are lost, Foreigners encroach upon us, the Poor are starv'd and the like.

"Whereas the sum of the matter is, the Manufacturer went mad . . . and when the trade stops a little he runs aground, so the Poor are starving and ready to mutiny for want of work: And this we call a Decay of Trade, whereas the contrary is true several ways. Trade must certainly decay, if we will run it up to such a length as to make more goods than the world can consume. But 'tis not to be justly called a decay of trade, 'tis only abating of the Flood, the waters were out, and now they were down again and reduced to their old channel." Such an accident, he says, was the plague in France (in 1720) which transferred demand from French to English goods. On such occasions "the manufacturers have made their good fortune a Bubble upon themselves and having overrun the market with their goods it returns upon them like the late South Sea, and every thing goes back from its imaginary to its intrinsick value. The demand abates the advancement, the Price sinks; the poor spinners and workfolk are dismissed to starve, the market is perhaps glutted for a year or more to come. . . .

"I remember after the late plague in France and the Peace in Spain [at Seville, 1729 ?] the Run for goods was so great in England and the Price of everything rose so high that the poor women in Essex could earn one shilling to one shilling and sixpence *per diem* by spinning. What was the consequence, 'twas too plain to be concealed. The poor farmers could get no dary maids, the wenches told them in so many words they would not go to service for twelve pence a week, when they could get nine shillings a week at their own hands as they called it. So they all run away to Bocking, to Sudbury, to Braintree and to Colchester and other manufacturing towns in Essex and Suffolk. The very Plowmen did the same. . . . As soon as the demand slack'd from abroad all these loose people were turn'd off, the spinsters went to begging, the weavers rose in rebellion. . . . "[1]

It was, presumably, the way in which whole districts were plunged into unemployment on some check to the local industry which gave rise to the general, but almost certainly mistaken, belief that the introduction of manufactures into a district, though it might, in the common phrase "employ the poor," yet always brought poverty and an intolerable burden of poor rates. Irregular employment was of three kinds. There was "deadness of trade" (a recurrent complaint) due to a commercial or political crisis, over-production, or some change in fashion or demand. And in so far as production was in the hands of small men things were made worse as contemporaries well knew, witness a comparison of the wool and the silk industries in 1719: "The clothier in the country goes on as long as he can get credit for a bag of wooll to work on or a peny to pay his

[1] *A Plan of the English Commerce*, 2nd Ed., 1730, p. 257 ff.

workmen . . . but in Spitalfields the case alters, there the manufacturers are near the market, they do not put the wooll or silk to spinning, but buy it in the yarn: as soon as the market stops they stop. If they cannot sell their work they immediately knock off the looms, and the journeymen as immediately starve." Starvation was periodic among the Spitalfields silk-weavers in the eighteenth century.[1]

When the small producer who worked at home for a middleman or a merchant found the prices of his goods falling, his only resource was to redouble his efforts and throw his goods—even below their prime cost—on a falling market, depressing prices still more. And while the small employer or middleman cut off his orders altogether, the large employer could afford to make for stock and wait for an improving market. The increase in size of industrial undertakings as the century went on was a steadying influence: One of the many advantages of English over French manufactures at the time of the Anglo-French commercial treaty of 1786, as set forth in a bitter complaint from the Normandy Chamber of Com-

[1] See M. D. George, *London Life in the Eighteenth Century*, pp. 179, 193.

merce, was the " great advantage enjoyed by the English from the accumulation of capital in the hands of their manufacturers and from the credit of their merchants. This allows them " to keep their men constantly employed even when trade is accidentally interrupted by the saturation of the markets." In France, in such a case, manufacturers are obliged to discharge their men, so that when the crisis is over orders cannot be executed.[1]

The second type of unemployment was seasonal. This was general in most trades. Seaborne trade before the days of steam was usually seasonal and always irregular. Sometimes the Thames was so crowded with shipping that the lightermen, waterside workers and even the Custom-house men were quite unable to deal with it. Sometimes a contrary wind kept the Pool of London almost empty.

Seasonal unemployment was so much the rule in London that schoolmastering, in the schools attended by artisans' children paying perhaps threepence a week (and these belonged to the aristocracy of labour), was a seasonal occupation. Assistants were taken on to deal with an influx of children in the summer; when their parents fell

[1] Prof. Sée in the *Economic History Review*, Jan. 1930, p. 312.

out of work as winter approached, the children stopped going to school and the assistants were dismissed.

There was also the day to day and week to week irregularity which was inherent in the domestic or putting-out system. Work had to be given out and returned and there was, almost inevitably, waiting between job and job. And as work was not as a rule paid for till it was finished, the workman was apt to be either in debt to his employer, or (in towns) a slave to the pawnshop. To quote from a pamphlet concerned with London workmen: "The weavers, taylors, shoemakers, and most other mechanical trades . . . now lose two days in every six . . . the greatest part whereof is lost thro' an idle or some other vicious inclination: some part . . . is lost for want of work. A great part of their time is spent in fetching home their materials, or carrying home their work, or in seeking after their money. . . . "

In spite of this recurrent and inevitable unemployment there was, in the earlier part of the century, a most unsympathetic attitude towards the distress arising from it, and this is one reason why we know comparatively little about it. Defoe is illuminating, both on the normal irregularity of employment and on the attitude towards it: "When wages are good they won't work any more than from hand to mouth; or if they do work they spend it in riot or luxury, so that it turns to no account to them. Again as soon as trade receives a check, and there is a little discouragement upon the clothiers and manufacturers so that work is a little stop'd and the masters and employers can give no wool out to spin, or perhaps but a little, and that in consequence of this the price abates too; what follows? Why then they grow clamorous and noisy, mutinous and saucy another way, and in the meantime they disperse, run away, and leave their families upon the parishes, and wander about in beggary and distress."[1]

The worker had to be blamed for idleness, that was common form, but it is a fact that contemporary accounts of the old domestic worker, both favourable and unfavourable, agree that if he could earn enough to live upon in three days he would enjoy himself for the rest of the week, probably in an alehouse. He had also a perfectly understandable preference for times of leisure compensated by days and nights of excessive toil. He would keep Saint Monday, as the saying went,

[1] *The Behaviour of Servants*, 1724, pp. 88–9.

possibly Saint Tuesday, and then perhaps work all night at the end of the week. And though this may have been all very well for the man it must have been exasperating for his wife and very bad for the children and apprentices (if he had any) who helped with his work.

In the illustration journeymen are keeping Saint Monday. The scene is an alehouse; the clock shows that it is four minutes to three. Two tailors sit side by side on a bench, one is singing " a New Song " from a broadside. Another man reads the *Daily Public Advertiser*. Other workmen are playing a game of cards watched by bystanders, and a quarrel is in progress—a bricklayer flourishes his trowel in anger. A painter is dead drunk—large tankards—' quart pots '—are much in evidence. The hostess is chalking up a score. Women come in to see if they can get money from their husbands or induce them to go back to work. An employer looks into the room through a window to see if there is any chance of getting his men to return to work.

A London doctor describes workmen as alternately working hard and drinking hard. " . . . always idle," he says, " when they have any money left, so that their life is spent between labour and attention above their powers, and perfect idleness and drunkenness." This was thought to be inherent in the English character, and the classic pronouncement on the subject is that of Defoe: "We are the most *lazy-diligent* nation in the world. . . . There is nothing more frequent than for an Englishman to work till he has got his pockets full of money, and then go and be idle or perhaps drunk till 'tis all gone and perhaps himself in debt. . . . Ask him in his cups what he intends. He'll tell you honestly, he'll drink so long as it lasts, and then go to work for more." Without venturing on the dangerous ground of national character, one can hardly doubt that much of this was due to environment—the natural result of irregular employment, irregular payment, little scope for the spending of money outside the alehouse, and, comparatively speaking, a low standard of living—though it was universally agreed that this was much higher in England than on the Continent. It was this ingrained habit of irregular work which made the tyranny of the factory bell so hateful to the first generation of factory workers. The disposition to earn no more than a bare subsistence had important consequences. It produced a deep conviction that steady work was done only when wages were low or food dear, and that consequently, high wages were disastrous to English trade, not merely because of the lower wages elsewhere (it was sometimes admitted—or claimed—that the Englishman did more work in a day than the Frenchman or the Dutchman) but because high wages meant drinking, and the impossibility of getting work done. The most skilled and most highly paid men were, it was said, the most idle. Of course, there were men who were highly skilled, highly paid and industrious, but since sobriety and steadiness had then a scarcity value, their reward was correspondingly high, a fact which goes some way to explain Wesley's remark: "Industry and frugality cannot but produce riches." This is by the way. Though we hear so much about high wages and idleness, since most pamphlets were written from the employer's point of view, the really striking thing about the old system is the great length of the normal working day and also the excessive toil which was the outcome sometimes of low piece-rate wages, sometimes of intermittent unemployment, voluntary and involuntary. Francis Place was, in his early days, a journeyman breeches maker in London. His wife helped with the work which was given out by his employer, and they lived, worked and slept, as was common in London, in a single room. After eight months' unemployment, due to a strike, in which they nearly starved, he got a plentiful supply of work. "We now," he says, "worked full 16, and sometimes 18, hours a day, Sundays and all. I never went out of the house for many weeks, and could not find time for a month to shave myself." Thus their household goods were redeemed from the pawnshop. The voluntary idleness of which we hear so much must surely have been due, not only to the economic organization of the domestic system, which made for irregularity, but also to the deadly monotony of very long hours of work in what was called the home. Here again Francis Place is illuminating. "I know not how to describe," he says, "the sickening aversion which at times steals over the working man and utterly disables him, for a longer or shorter period, from following his usual occupation, and compels him to indulge in *idleness.* I have felt it, resisted it to the utmost of my power, but have been obliged to submit and run away from my work. This is the case with every workman I have ever known. . . . The best informed among the workmen will, occasionally, solace themselves at such times with liquor, the uninformed will almost always recur to the same means to procure the excitement which must be procured."

It so happens that a domestic worker—a stocking-weaver or framework knitter from his apprenticeship in 1737 till about 1750—has left a record of his life, written with transparent honesty. This is William Hutton; his career as a framework knitter is only not typical, because, from the smallest possible beginnings, he managed to build up a bookseller's business and so escape from his hated trade. His father was a Derby wool-comber, neither "sober, for he spent all he could get in liquor, nor clean, for his trade was oily." Employment at the earliest possible age "for the benefit of the family" was the natural lot of his children. William, at the age of seven, in 1730, was condemned to the famous Derby silk mill[1], the first textile factory in England. It is interesting to find that out of three hundred he was "by far the least and the youngest." "I had now," he says, "to rise at five every morning during seven years, submit to the cane whenever convenient to the master; be the constant companion of the most rude and vulgar of the human race. . . ." "The

[1] See below, p. 146.

THE ART OF STOCKING—FRAME-WORK—KNITTING, 1750

confinement and labour were no burden," a saying which throws a painful light on the common and accepted lot of the poor. He adds, "but the severity was intolerable." He lived at home, but was indentured for seven years. This was a blind alley employment, and at the end of it his permanent trade had to be chosen and a second term of apprenticeship begun. As usual, the choice was the father's, not the son's. The boy wanted to be a gardener, but he was bound to his uncle, a stocking-weaver, though this was known to be a "starving trade." But the father was dilatory, the uncle was pressing since his livelihood chiefly depended on the earnings of his apprentices.

William's task as an apprentice was to earn five shillings a week for his master. The first time he accomplished this "stint" (which was at the end of a few months) he was rewarded with sixpence, but having once done this if he fell short of the stint, he was in debt to his master by the amount of the deficiency; what he earned above it was for himself, and out of this problematical surplus his clothes had to be bought. In his second year he was "put to the fine frame" and had to earn 6s. 9d. a week. Apprentices were generally under the mark, and the burden of over-work in order to get clothes he found intolerable. However, with one attempt at freedom, when he ran away for a week but was driven back by starvation, he served out his time and became his uncle's journeyman. He was skilful and exceptionally industrious and in seven years he had managed to earn seven pounds; "I had served two seven years to two trades, neither of which I could subsist upon." The thought of remaining a journeyman in this wretched trade was unbearable and he proposed to become a master, "though of the very lowest order," by hiring a frame and putting it in his uncle's workshop for the usual rent of a standing; he would then work for a stocking warehouse. His uncle refused, though, Hutton says, the terms were common and would have been accepted anywhere. The next year, 1746, he borrowed £10 from a brother-in-law and bought a frame. The sequel was tragic: "The stocking frame being my own, and trade being dead, the hosiers would not employ me. They could scarce employ their own frames. I was advised to try Leicester, and took with me half a dozen pair of stockings to sell. I visited several warehouses; but alas! all proved blank. They would neither employ me, nor give for my goods any thing near prime cost. I was so affected, that I burst into tears, to think that I should have served seven years to a trade at which I could not get my bread."

This is a striking picture of the toils of apprenticeship as well as of the weak position of the small master in a domestic industry when trade was 'dead' in the significant metaphor of the age. His desperate efforts to earn a living only resulted in glutting the market. Hutton's story had a happy ending because by incredible industry he managed to build up a successful business as a bookseller in Birmingham. He was encouraged to take the first rash step (in 1749) because, he says, "if I continued at the frame, I was certain to be poor; and if I ventured to leave it, I could but be so." Moreover, "I had observed such severe penury among the married stockingers, that the thoughts of a wife were horrid. . . . " In his prosperous old age, his daughter relates, he used to say, "How thankful ought I to be for the comforts that surround me. Where should I have been now if I had continued a stockinger? I must have been in the workhouse. They all go there when they cannot see to work."

Nevertheless, in the early nineteenth century, there was the inevitable legend of prosperity in the trade in the good old days of the eighteenth century: " Every village had its wake, in Leicestershire, the lower orders lived at comparative ease and plenty, having right of common for pig and poultry and sometimes for a cow. The stocking makers each had a garden, a barrel of home-brewed ale, a week-day suit of clothes and one for Sundays and plenty of leisure, seldom working more than three days a week."[1]

Nevertheless, the workhouse, " when they cannot see to work," was their fate.

The poor house in old age seems to have been the common lot of the industrial worker, as it was of the agricultural labourer, when he had not, as many had, improved his position in the world. It was another domestic worker, a Sheffield file-hewer, who wrote the bitter *File-hewers Lamentation:*

> My trade and occupation,
> Was ground for Lamentation,
> Which makes me curse my station,
> And wish I'd ne'er been born.
>
> * * *
>
> I ne'er can save one shilling
> And must—which is more killing
> A pauper die when old.[2]

[1] Gardner, *Music and Friends*, ii, 810.

[2] Lloyd, G. I. H., *The Cutlery Trades*, 1913.

CHAPTER IV

THE MIDDLE YEARS, OR THE NEW HUMANITARIANISM

THE middle years of the eighteenth century were years of crisis for England. The period round about 1750 and 1760 which looms so large in accounts of the industrial revolution does mark a turning point in social history. Developments in religion, literature, science, industry, politics, were all acting and reacting on one another and preparing the way for the modern world. A change came over that mysterious thing, the spirit of the age.

We can regard the eighteenth century as an age of corruption, oligarchy, privilege, materialism, or we can regard it as an age of common sense, good humour, reasonableness and toleration—one view does not exclude the other. Above all things, enthusiasm was regarded with horror, though it is fair to say that enthusiasm was then identified with fanaticism. On an eighteenth-century tombstone was inscribed as the highest of praise, 'pious without enthusiasm.' But with the middle of the century things were changing fast. The great religious revival of Wesley and Whitefield was a spiritual revolution comparable with the revolution in industry, and it cuts right across these notions of the age. In its early stages Methodism was highly emotional, it gave rise to hysteria, and in fact it was the very embodiment of enthusiasm; it was intolerant, for instance, it obstructed the coming of Catholic Emancipation. It was puritanical in its gospel of unremitting work and its distrust of all amusement. In the school which Wesley founded at Kingswood for the children of miners, the pupils got up, winter and summer, at 4; they were to sing, to pray, to meditate, to walk, but on no account to play, for "he that plays when he is a child will play when he is a man." On the other hand, Methodism repudiated that undue respect for wealth with which the puritans are often reproached. Wesley was fully conscious of the deceitfulness of riches. He said, "I do not see how it is possible in the nature of things for a religious revival to last long. For religion must necessarily produce industry and frugality. And these cannot but produce riches. But as Riches increase, so will Pride and love of the world in all its branches."

With the growth of Methodism and emotional religion there was a decline of the scepticism, free-thought and barren controversy which had dominated the earlier years of the century. And Methodism was a democratic movement, which does not of course mean that Wesley was not a Tory. Its chief appeal was in the industrial towns, among miners and in sea-ports, where it was a great civilizing and educating influence. Its influence spread far outside its own congregations and gave rise to the evangelical movement in the Church of England. It was an important current in the rising tide of humanitarianism, and one of the channels through which the Age of Reason merged in the Age of Feeling.

Politically, the new spirit was seen in the reaction against the cynical materialism and corruption associated (rightly or wrongly) with Walpole's long administration. The new patriotism was personified in Pitt, and was stimulated by military success —by the 'wonderful year' of Minden and Quebec. And Pitt, like Wesley, is significant of the stirrings of democracy. When he became head of the Government in 1757 (though not nominally prime minister) it was in spite of the king and in spite of the family arrangements which then dominated politics. Pitt got his position because he was popular and he was popular because he stood for a new spirit in politics—opposition to corruption—hitherto the monopoly of Opposition. A popular minister was a new thing in English history. As Dr. Johnson put it, Walpole was a minister given by the king to the people. Pitt was a minister given by the people to the king.

Between the appearance of Richardson's *Pamela* in 1740, and Sterne's *Tristram Shandy* in 1760, the novel came into its own and established itself as concerned with the lives and the psychology of actual human beings. And in Fielding's hands it at once became an instrument of social reform. With Sterne the conversion of the age to sentiment was effected, enthusiasm almost ceased to be a term of reproach, sentiment became the fashion. These literary developments are connected with the increasing influence of the middle class, and like Methodism they are a factor in the new humanitarianism.

By a strange concidence, this development of the novel was brought into direct as well as indirect relation with social history through Henry Fielding.

His appointment as a salaried justice of the peace for Westminster in 1749 was in its way as epoch-making as the appearance of *Tom Jones* in the same year. He was succeeded at Bow Street in 1754 by his half-brother the blind Sir John, who ruled there till his death in 1780. Out of Bow Street developed the police court, on the lines laid down by the Fieldings. Indeed, the traditions of the modern police court, as the poor man's court of justice, derive directly from Bow Street and the Fieldings. In their day the court was what it is now, a court of conciliation, a place where the poor could get free advice on points of law. It is worth noting that the practice of collecting funds for hard cases coming to the notice of the magistrates was begun by Henry Fielding. He was the first of a succession of London magistrates who were active social reformers with an expert knowledge of the difficulties of the poor. The old sort of London magistrate had preyed on the poor, the new sort protected the poor.

Pitt, Wesley and Fielding were portents of a new age and a more democratic one. Everywhere changes were going on which prepared the way for the modern world. A most significant and fundamental change began about 1750. The population, which till then had increased very slowly, began to increase fast. The chief cause of this was a fall in the death-rate, which had been appallingly high, especially in towns and above all in London. The statistics are very faulty, but about the main facts there can be no doubt. In towns deaths exceeded births and yet the towns continued to grow. It was clear that they grew only at the expense of the healthier country districts ; London in particular was regarded as a devouring monster. It was even supposed that in this way the population of the whole country was falling fast. Though the pessimists were wrong, the seriousness of the waste of life as it was called was apparent. The crux of the matter was infant mortality, which was ghastly, especially among the children of the poor and was worst of all among poor-law children in workhouses or entrusted to the care of nurses paid by the parish—creatures compared with whom Mrs. Gamp would have been almost a ministering angel. This dreadful waste of life was the starting-point of a movement for reform which directed itself first of all against the traffic in gin. There is a familiar story of the London signboard inviting customers to be drunk for a penny, dead drunk for twopence, with clean straw for a halfpenny. This was an example of sardonic London humour, not (as is usually supposed) a common legend on signboards, but it would be impossible to exaggerate the horrors of the great gin-drinking period which was at its worst between 1720 and 1750 when the death-rate was also at its highest. Distilling had been encouraged by the Government as a remedy for the over-production of corn which was then thought to be a danger to the whole agricultural interest. "The distillers are the farmers' great friends," said a pamphleteer in 1736, "what would become of our corn *injured by bad harvests* were it not for the Distillers?"[1] But the over-production of gin (which was very cheap, fiery and poisonous) was found to be threatening the very existence of the race, and there was a succession of Acts to check the consumption of spirits. It is interesting to note that one (in 1736) which amounted practically to prohibition was a complete failure—it led to riot and murder and could not be enforced. So the attempt was given up and the method adopted which has been followed more or less ever since to make spirits dearer and to make the conditions of sale decent. A beginning

[1] W. Allen, *Ways and Means to raise the Value of Land*

was made on these lines in 1751, and after this spirit drinking declined, crimes of violence diminished and health improved.

The campaign against gin is important not only because it was effective, but because it was one of the first attempts to get a measure of social reform by putting pressure on Parliament. Petitions from doctors, magistrates and industrial towns were backed up by press propaganda. Fielding wrote a famous pamphlet on the connection between drink, crime and poverty. Hogarth published his *Gin Lane* engraving which depicts a scene in the parish of St. Giles. In all this there was nothing whatever of the spirit of temperance reform—that movement was not yet born. It was thought to be one of the evils of gin (as of tea) that it interfered with the consumption of beer.

The decline of spirit drinking had a direct effect on the death-rate and especially on infant mortality. Another cause of improvement was an advance in medical knowledge and especially in midwifery. The middle of the century was a great period for the founding of hospitals. Those of the Middle Ages had been intended for places of refuge for the sick poor. With the Elizabethan poor law, the sick became the care of the parish, and it was part of the duty of the parish workhouse, or poor house, when there was one, to be an infirmary. The idea behind the hospital movement of the eighteenth century was that hospitals would be centres for acquiring and spreading medical knowledge. And so they were. Five great London hospitals were founded between 1720 and 1745, the first by Guy the bookseller, the others by bodies of subscribers. The movement spread to the provinces; indeed, Dr. Addenbrooke's Hospital at Cambridge was founded the year before Guy's. But since hygiene and sanitation were in their infancy, hospitals in these early days must not be credited with too direct a share in the saving of life. Pictures of eighteenth-century hospitals show the patients two in a bed, which can have been neither healthy nor comfortable. Still, workhouses were far worse. For instance, Shoreditch parish complained that their workhouse was so crowded that 39 children had to sleep in three beds. Typhus in those days was called indiscriminately gaol fever or hospital fever. Wooden bedsteads with testers were breeding places for the vermin which carried the disease. At the end of the century iron beds, a by-product of the industrial revolution, began to be introduced to the great advantage of health.

The next stage was an enormous advance in midwifery which was connected with the establishment of maternity hospitals and lying-in charities at which both doctors and midwives were trained. Then came the dispensary movement, which set up centres where the poorer people could attend for medicine and advice while those who could not attend were visited in their homes. These things began in London and were initiated elsewhere. Dr. Lettsom, a famous London doctor, said in 1775 that in a very few years, as a result of dispensaries, he had observed a total revolution in the conduct of the common people respecting their diseased friends; "they have learnt," he said, "that most diseases are mitigated by a free admission of air, by cleanliness and by promoting instead of restraining the indulgence and care of the sick." The doctors on their side learned to diagnose the diseases of poverty and dirt. Industrial disease, especially the consequence of lead poisoning, began to receive attention. This was only a beginning, but the advance from almost zero was immense. The effect on the death-rate was striking. England at this time owed a great deal to doctors as well as to magistrates.

Joseph Hanway, a city merchant, now chiefly

known for having introduced the use of the umbrella, did wonders for parish children by getting an Act[1] to make it compulsory that London parishes should send infants into the country to be nursed. The effect on infant mortality was remarkable, and it is an important landmark because it was the beginning of a movement for greater generosity in matters of poor-relief—it was intended not, like earlier Acts, to check extravagance, but to prevent 'undue parsimony' in parish officers.

We are often told that nothing was done for the health of towns till after 1842. But, from the 60's of the eighteenth century onwards, first London and then other towns carried out improvement schemes for paving, lighting, draining and pulling down ruinous and obstructive buildings. These had a very great effect on health, though civic improvement was their first object. The result was that some ghastly slums which had survived from Tudor and Stuart times as well as much that was picturesque disappeared. The chief London streets which Dr. Johnson in the 40's had called fit for a colony of Hottentots, became the admiration of Europe. In the 80's the pavements, the street lamps, the water supply

[1] In 1769.

and the sewers of London were regarded as marvels. It is worth noting that foreign visitors were deeply impressed with the safety of foot-passengers in London. They saw in this an outcome of English liberty: "Their laws," they say, "are not made and executed entirely by people who always ride in chariots." The Prince of Monaco when he arrived on a visit to George III thought the ordinary lights were a special illumination in his honour. Of course, by modern standards, London was then dark, dingy and extremely insanitary.

Other towns improved, too, and there was a remarkable improvement in the health of Manchester during a period in which the population increased fourfold. The new washable cottons which were universally worn by women replaced such things as linsey-woolsey petticoats padded with horsehair or cotton wool, and leather stays, worn till they dropped to pieces from dirt. And the change in dress did what Francis Place calls "almost marvels" for the health and cleanliness of women.

The improvement in health, though it was greatest in towns, where things had been worse, affected the whole country. Marshes were drained as a result of canal making and land reclamation, and agues and fevers diminished. Improvement was most marked between 1780 and 1815—that is, during the first onslaught of industrialism and during a great war which brought with it violent fluctuations of trade and other evils. How can this be explained, and above all, how can it be reconciled with the poverty and distress of which we hear on all sides ?

Crudely, one may say that bad as things were they had been worse before—at all events so far as health was concerned. For various reasons we know a great deal about the distresses of this period, very little about earlier periods, though there are abundant indications of misery and wretchedness if we choose to look for them. But there was now a new attitude to suffering of all kinds.

The miseries of slaves, of prisoners, great cruelty to animals, for instance, had long been taken for granted, but were now beginning to seem intolerable. The medieval and monastic rule for the bringing up of children—that they should be 'confined and chastised'—was gradually being discredited, though it held its ground in the traditional treatment of apprentices. The savage penal laws were criticized and less ferociously administered.

The new humanitarianism was not without its critics. And as the assertion that there was relaxation in the administration of the criminal laws in the eighteenth century may provoke scepticism, one of the most uncompromising of these critics may be quoted. This was Sir John Hawkins, Dr. Johnson's unclubbable friend. "We live in an age when humanity is in fashion, . . . " he wrote in 1787, " there was a time when as well prisoners for debt as other offences, were cruelly treated . . . but at this day, the temper of the times is under a contrary bias, for, not only in actual confinement are prisoners treated with greater lenity than till of late years was ever known, but, in courts of justice, the regard shown to offenders falls little short of respect. In prosecutions at the suit of the Crown, the indulgence of prisoners is nearly as great as it ought to be, were that true which the law does but hardly presume, *viz.* that every offender who is brought to legal trial, is innocent till his guilt be proved. Those whose duty it is to conduct the evidence, fearing the censure that others have received by a contrary treatment of prisoners, are restrained from enforcing it, and, as it is an exercise that costs nothing, it is sure to gain the applause of the vulgar." He goes on to enumerate fifteen chances which may save a criminal from the gallows; the comment of Porson that he gives "proofs that every prisoner ought to be convicted and every convict hanged" is scarcely an exaggeration.

Hawkins was a London magistrate—for many years chairman of the Middlesex Sessions, and he was filled with a consuming jealousy of Bow Street. Hatred made him clear-sighted enough to recognize the part played by the Fielding tradition, both in literature and at Bow Street, in the new spirit he so much resented. "Fielding's morality," he says (as expressed in *Tom Jones*), "in respect that it resolves virtue into good affections in contradiction to moral obligations and a sense of duty, is that of Lord Shaftesbury vulgarized, and is a system of excellent use in palliating the vices most injurious to society. He was the inventor of that cant phrase, goodness of heart, which is every day used as a substitute for probity and means little more than the virtue of a horse or a dog; in short, he has done more towards corrupting the rising generation than any writer we know of."

The new humanitarianism, whose most striking achievement was the abolition of the slave trade, carried through (in 1804) in spite of war and in spite of political reaction, had many blind spots. It lends itself to irony, but if we cultivate a historical point of view it will seem more reasonable to regard it as an advance on the past than to blame it for failing to reach standards which were still in the future. Its result in our period was a number of reforms, often forgotten, small in scope as compared with what came after but very important as the manifestation of a new spirit and new methods. It resulted in a number of enquiries into social conditions, some by individuals, some by the Government, some by the philanthropic societies which were springing up in all directions. These revealed a mass of misery which had long existed but was often supposed to be new.

Then there is much evidence of a rise in the standard of living and intelligence among all but the poorest of the workers. This was often called the growth of luxury and the decay of subordination. As Dr. Johnson deplored, it is "sadly broken down in this age. No man, now, has the authority his father had, except a gaoler." And, as a matter of fact, as Hawkins knew, even the gaoler was no longer the licensed and brutal tyrant he had been.

The discontent of the workers found expression in newspapers and pamphlets, and in meetings, public and private. But the teaching of history as well as of common sense and common experience is that articulate discontent is no evidence of a decline in prosperity or status. Active propaganda and most legitimate grievances brought a minority of the humbler classes into conflict with the deplorable political reaction which resulted from the French Revolution, when Jacobins and republicans were at least as much dreaded as Bolsheviks have been in our day. And people sometimes assume that political reaction is inconsistent with social betterment.

I do not mean to suggest that this was a time of unchequered social advance. The agricultural labourer had been excluded from his share of agricultural prosperity and had been deeply—though not deliberately—wronged. There are evils which are not to be measured by statistics of wages or even of health. But the evils of industrialism are so obvious that it behoves us the more to recognise its compensations. The rapid transformation of agricultural workers into industrial workers was fraught with evil consequences, but they were not all evil. And the agricultural labourer of the eighteenth century as of the twentieth was in many cases eager for the transformation. Francis Place, who regarded a cotton mill with such horror that he refused even to see one, always insisted on the great benefits to the working classes of new industrial developments. "The progress made in refinement of manners and morals seems to have gone on simultaneously with the improvement in arts, manufactures and commerce," he wrote in his *Autobiography*.[1]

It is important to realize that those who were most conscious of living in an age of progress did not measure it only in terms of production and inventions—in cotton exports and steam engines. In 1816 Rickman, who was responsible for the early census returns, wrote to the poet Southey: "One thing I wish to say as to an opinion you entertain as to the well-being or rather ill-being of the poor, that their state has grown worse and worse of late. Now, if one listens to common assertion, everything in grumbling England grows worse and worse; but the fact in question is even a curiosity. Human comfort is to be estimated by human health, and that by the length of human life. . . . Since 1780 life has been prolonged by

[1] See M. D. George, *London Life*, p. 4.

5 to 4—and the poor form too large a portion of society to be excluded from this general effect; rather they are the main cause of it; for the upper classes had food and cleanliness abundant before."

CHAPTER V

THE VILLAGE IN TRANSITION

THE middle of the eighteenth century is a turning point in the history of agriculture as of industry. Each was undergoing changes which were reacting on the other and on society at large, and though in both cases these changes were only the speeding up of processes that had long been going on, they were truly revolutionary. The form of rural England as it is to-day, with its roads (motor-roads of course excepted), is largely the result of happenings in a critical period between about 1760 and 1815. The central point of this agricultural revolution was the enclosure of the old open-field villages which had survived from the Middle Ages. The changes have a poignant interest because, in the early nineteenth century, disaster fell upon the village. How far was this a result of the agricultural revolution ? Controversy raged round the question of enclosures in the eighteenth century and rages round it still—it has obscured as well as illuminated the problem. In the past the controversy became acute in times of dearth and distress, and the controversialists were apt to put the blame for hard times on everything they disliked: enclosures, rich farmers, dealers in corn, speculators, the consumption of tea, luxury—a vague and question-begging term.

The controversy in the eighteenth century was confused by a belief that the population was shrinking fast, while actually it was increasing faster than ever before. Two things gave rise to the belief: a fall in the number of deaths—due really to the fall in the death-rate: secondly, a decline in the exportation of corn. About 1773 England ceased to be a corn-exporting country on a large scale. This was really due to the increased consumption of a larger population: an increased demand for wheaten bread instead of bread made partly or entirely of rye, barley, or oats; and to an enormous increase in the number of horses due to improved transport. But the decline in deaths and corn exports was explained as due to "depopulation and luxury," and it was argued that this imaginary decline in the population and food supply was due to enclosures. As usual there were the exceptional cases which could be cited in support of an unsound generalization. The well-known line in Goldsmith's *Deserted Village:* "Where wealth accumulates and men decay," sums up the contentions of a number of dreary pamphlets. But though in most cases the population of villages increased after enclosures as the food supply certainly did, the number of farms was often lessened.

The enclosures of the sixteenth and early seventeenth centuries had been for sheep-farming and the production of wool, and did definitely lead to depopulation. The enclosures of the eighteenth century were for improved agriculture—for mixed farming and an improved rotation in which the crops provided food for stock, and more stock produced manure for more crops and better crops. Thus the supply of wheat was increased, and sheep were bred for mutton rather than wool, while they were valued by the farmer chiefly as producing manure for cereals. Moreover by the new Norfolk rotation and turnip cultivation sandy wastes were turned into rich arable land. This was a revolution in agriculture.

Broadly speaking, enclosures were an economic necessity—England had to produce more food: in war time the alternative was starvation. But they were carried out largely at the expense of the small farmer and without regard for the moral claims of the poor. Before discussing the losses and gains of enclosure, it will be well to remind ourselves what the old system was like. Where the open-field village had survived from the Middle Ages, all the arable land was divided into great fields, usually three: one sown with wheat, one with some variety of spring corn, one was always fallow. This was the three-field rotation. Each owner or tenant had his holding made up of a number of strips scattered widely through the three fields, so that no one should have an undue share of fallow in any one year. Parts of the holding were bound to be far from the farm buildings which were all collected together in the village, so that the labour of ploughing and carrying was great. In an extreme case in Gloucestershire one acre was in eight portions and to visit them meant a walk of two or three miles. In spite of the wasteful fallow every third year much of the land was exhausted from repeated grain crops. In many places methods of agriculture had even deteriorated since the Middle Ages with their highly organized manorial economy and the coercion involved in villeinage. The practice of marling, for instance, had fallen into disuse.

Each village had its common and waste—heath, marsh or woodland—which had never been taken in from the wild. On this the holders of land in the village farm had the right of pasturing their beasts and gathering fuel. Cottagers with little or no land had also varying rights of common: these might be anything from the right of cutting turf, gathering brushwood or grazing geese to that of pasturing sheep or cows. Sometimes a fee was paid to the lord of the manor for each beast on the common. There were also permanent enclosures for hay; and after the grain harvest the farmers had the right of pasturing beasts on the stubble—a right which effectively prevented the introduction of a new rotation.

For centuries the enclosure of open fields had been going on—by agreement, purchase, force or fraud. The strips had been sorted out and exchanged and turned into compact farms, the wastes had been steadily shrinking by encroachment and cultivation. Thus the great bare furrowed tracts had been transformed into fields intersected by lanes as we know them to-day. Compact holdings had been carved out of the waste. Farmhouses had been built on enclosed farms. In some parts of England the open-field system had never existed. Where agriculture was most advanced, as in Kent, the country had been enclosed very early. Fruit-growing, dairy-farming, root crops and hop-growing needed enclosures. Round London very advanced methods had been introduced: the milk producers and graziers of the neighbouring districts had perfected the growing of hay. Fruit and flower-growing and nursery-gardening were very highly developed by the early eighteenth century. In fact, at that time England seems to have been in advance of France: such things as cauliflowers and asparagus were forced under bell-glasses; vegetables such as broccoli were eaten in the public houses while they were still rare in France.[1] But close to this advanced cultivation there were still large areas in open fields and the commons and wastes round London were regarded as a nuisance since they were the haunt of highwaymen.

The open fields which still remained to be enclosed lay chiefly in a great central wedge across England from Dorset in the south-west to York-

[1] Le Blanc, *Letters on the English and French Nations*, 1741, i, 319.

shire in the north-east. In the eighteenth century enclosures were chiefly carried out by private Acts of Parliament procured by the richer landowners. They were very unpopular with the small farmers and cottagers. For a long time writers on agriculture had been pointing out how wasteful and slovenly a thing was open-field farming—"this mingle mangle," as an old writer called it—how it gave rise to quarrels, the prevailing sin being the removal of a neighbour's landmark. Not only was the breeding of improved stock impossible but infectious disease played havoc among the beasts who roamed at large, while on undrained commons rot was a prevalent disease among the sheep. Cattle were valued for the length of bone and strength of sinew which enabled them to extricate themselves from bogs.

These things had long been known and deplored, and much land had been enclosed. In the early eighteenth century root crops and artificial grasses were introduced which could not be grown on open fields; these did away with the need for the wasteful fallow every third year and enormously improved the methods of breeding stock and manuring land. The new mixed farming meant more and better crops and more and better stock.

Among the great names in this phase of agricultural innovation are those of Jethro Tull, a gentleman farmer who began life as a lawyer, Lord Townshend (Turnip Townshend) a great Norfolk landlord, and Robert Bakewell a Leicestershire farmer and a typical John Bull. The last entertained the celebrities of Europe in his kitchen with such open-handed hospitality that he became bankrupt. The pioneers were followed by many others—experimenting landlords and practising farmers. Agriculture became a passion in Europe as well as in England. Arthur Young went on his famous tours and wrote of them with incomparable gusto. Though he failed as a practical farmer (in Suffolk, in Essex, and in Hertford where he took a 300 acre holding which he afterwards paid a farmer £100 to be quit of) he had a wide influence through his writings. Among the many amateur farmers who contributed to Young's justly famous *Annals of Agriculture* was George III, who wrote as Ralph Robinson. He not only superintended the home farm at Windsor but carved two experimental farms out of Windsor Great Park; rushy and even dangerous swamp and impoverished grass were transformed into two model farms, one cropped on the Flemish, the other on the Norfolk system. By a strange irony his subjects had complained that he neglected the business of state and the supervision of his ministers to amuse himself as Farmer George. A typical satire of 1771 depicts him as watching wind and weather through a telescope while state documents lie neglected on the ground.

In this age of agricultural enthusiasm, cattle shows, ploughing matches and farmers' clubs multiplied. The Society of Arts extended its encouragement to the inventors of agricultural improvements and scattered its medals among farmers and their wives. Agricultural societies came into existence: the Bath and West of England, the Smithfield Club, and most important, the Board of Agriculture with Sir John Sinclair as its president and Young as its secretary.

The question still remains, why was there this burst of agricultural enterprise and enthusiasm in the later eighteenth century? Why were there many more enclosure Acts after 1760 than before? Enclosure was expensive and speculative, and it was unpopular except with large landowners and a few farmers. While transport remained so bad that the farmer was restricted to a local market and the expense of procuring heavy manures was

FARMER GEORGE WATCHING WIND AND WEATHER

Oxford Magazine, 1771

[*face p.* 114

enormous, it could only be profitable in favoured places. In the early part of the century, low corn prices and bad roads made farming unprofitable, or so farmers and landlords said. So enclosures went on comparatively slowly till the economic demand became pressing. During the thirty-three years of George II's reign the average number of enclosure Acts in a year was seven, from 1760 to 1785 it was forty-seven, and from 1794 to 1804 it was seventy-eight. By 1760 244 enclosure Acts had been passed, by the end of the reign of George III, sixty years later, the total number was nearly 4000. This progressive increase reflects the increase in population, the growth of towns, "the growth of luxury," the improvement of transport, the pressure of war.

The complaints of atrocious roads are so poignant in the later eighteenth century that it is difficult to believe that anything good can be said of them before the days of Macadam. Still, even by 1750 turnpikes had done a good deal, freights were reduced because on improved roads fewer horses were needed, yet from this time onwards wheeled traffic increased so enormously that the number of horses in the country multiplied and the demand for grain increased. Driving became sometimes a pleasure instead of an intolerable fatigue. Johnson told Boswell that if he had no duties he would spend his life "in driving briskly in a post-chaise with a pretty woman." And Gibbon found driving a delightful "union of ease and motion." But compared with the best roads the bad ones seemed more intolerable than ever, as Arthur Young found when he toured in his south-country carriage on the roads of northern England. Enclosures and road improvement went on together. When land was enclosed portions were set aside for roads, which were fenced and drained. On open fields and across commons the high roads had been mere tracks, where the traveller was often lost—and where drivers encroached on cornfields to avoid dangerous ruts.

Still more important was the beginning of the age of canals. Canal making in England began late (though a good deal had been done to make rivers navigable), but when once it started it went on rapidly. When the first canal—built by Brindley for the Duke of Bridgewater from Worsley to Manchester—was opened in 1761 it was regarded as one of the wonders of the world with its barges riding aloft on an aqueduct.

Food prices rose with the increased demand and

THE DUKE OF BRIDGEWATER AND HIS CANAL

[*face p.* 116

when the farmer got a better market—not, as many people thought, as a result of enclosures, but enclosures multiplied when prices became higher. "Turnpike roads," it was said in 1772 (a year of commercial crisis and especially high prices), "enable the dealers in provisions to bring them at any season of the year to neighbouring towns and cities, which, if they can but effect they are almost certain of considerable profit. . . . The most fruitful parts of England before the roads were mended were natural magazines one half of the year, that is from November till May, the badness of the roads would not allow provisions to be brought from thence during that period ; the consequence was that manufactures were established in these places where labouring people could then afford to work reasonable, and the farmer or dairyman was willing to sell his produce in small quantities . . . these places are become populous by being manufactories, and thereby the inhabitants are become greatly distrest and miserable."[1]

Thus after 1760 enclosures were speeded up and were at their height between 1800 and 1815, in war-time, when corn-growing was both a patriotic

[1] T. Rooke, Esq., in *Political Register*, vi, 71, July 1772.

duty and extremely profitable. At this time land was brought under the plough which could be cultivated only when corn prices were very high. England had to produce more food or starve. More than once, with a bad harvest, famine came very near. In many ways the situation was like that in our war, with the great difference that in the twentieth century care was taken of the consumer by price-fixing and rationing. This would have been utterly beyond the administrative capacity of our ancestors. The wage-earner, too, was protected by wage boards; in the French wars he was handed over to the poor law—though in both periods many were raised above the need of either device by great increases in wages due to war conditions.

As in our war, it was necessary to bring more land under cultivation, and this necessarily followed from enclosure schemes which involved not only the rearrangement of the arable into compact fields but the enclosure and cultivation of the village waste. Nothing shows more clearly the difference between our over-industrialized country, dependent on imported food, and the England of the wars with France, than the attitude towards heaths and commons. The large extent of these was thought a disgrace to the country. Marshall, an agricultural expert, and a great authority, called them in 1801 " filthy blotches on the face of the country, especially when seen under the threatening clouds of famine which have now repeatedly overspread it." No one then dreamed of commons as playgrounds or lungs for town dwellers. They were regarded as a standing spectacle of sloth and agricultural backwardness, as a positive nuisance, and hideous into the bargain. They were too often the resort of highwaymen and sheep-stealers. When they were marshy, as they often were, they were a source of agues and fevers. The idea that a barren heath could be beautiful had not yet found favour, though people were beginning to admire mountains, and there was a positive craze for the picturesque —exemplified in ruins, real and artificial. Like many others, Defoe was scandalized at the wild state of Hindhead and the heaths of Surrey. A century later, Cobbett called Hindhead " certainly the most villainous spot that God ever made." The commoners would have deeply resented the idea that outsiders could have any rights on their common. These rights were as a rule in strict relation to their arable holdings or the tenure of certain cottages, and they were often paid for, either in rent or in fees for pasturage. They were sometimes less valuable than might appear, since rot and disease abounded among the animals turned out to graze.

As for the advantages of enclosure from the point of view of agriculture and food supply there can hardly be two opinions, in spite of occasional mistakes, and although the enthusiasts of the day sometimes overrated them.

Unfortunately, the social consequences were often deplorable, which does not mean that other and worse social evils might not have followed the continuation of the old methods. With the best of intentions it would have been difficult to prevent loss to the poorer villagers. Enclosures nearly always meant the elimination of the smaller holdings. They were intended to be a rationalizing of farming by getting rid of the less productive units—and these were the small open-field farmers who had always lived on the margin of poverty. The new methods could only be carried out on fair-sized farms, and they needed capital and enterprise. " These farmers," said a Northamptonshire petition against an enclosure Act, " know nothing of the grazing business, and they have not money to buy in a sufficient stock of cattle, much less to pay for an enclosure."[1] The amalgamation of farms was the natural consequence of an enclosure Act. Many small freeholders and copy holders however sold their land, rented large farms and prospered exceedingly. It has often been said that enclosures caused the extinction of the yeoman or small freeholder, but now it is generally thought that this was not so, and that during the time of rapid enclosure and farming prosperity their number actually increased, though doubtless with considerable changes among the individual holders.

The disappearance of many small farms meant that the displaced farmer had either to seek his living in a town or become a labourer. This must have meant many obscure tragedies. But it must not be forgotten that it was a tragedy which often happened, independently of enclosure. The poor-law records show that farmers often became labourers as labourers became farmers. In a hard and speculative occupation like that of the small farmer there were descents as well as ascents of the ladder. And the restricted markets and low prices so favourable to the growth of manufactures in the early part of the century were based on

[1] *Reasons humbly offered against the Bill for enclosing . . . the Common Fields in . . . Staverton. . . .* [Passed 1774.]

unprofitable farming. Many were the complaints of low rents and unpaid rents. " Innumerable are the distresses of our farmers," as William Allen said in 1736, " even among those who may be presumed to have good bargains." He believed that farming was suffering and would suffer from the over-production of corn. The grinding poverty of the small farmer was insisted on by a number of witnesses from Baxter onwards.[1]

" I am convinced," wrote Arthur Young, " that a day labourer, that is on an equality with the farmer in respect of children, is as well fed, as well clothed, and as well lodged as he would be, was he fixed in one of these little farms ; with this difference, that he does not work nearly so hard. Indeed, I regard these small occupiers as a set of very miserable men. They fare extremely hard, work without intermission like a horse—and practice every lesson of diligence and frugality without being able to soften their present lot. All the comfort they have, which the labourer does not possess, lies in the hope of increasing their little stock enough to take a larger farm ; but this does not happen so often as many people may imagine."[2]

[1] See above, p. 5.

[2] *The Farmer's Letters to the People of England*, 1767, p. 67.

The social virtue which the farmer possessed and the labourer did not, was that of thrift. Gilbert White describes how the frugal housewife made rushlights to save the cost of candles: "Little farmers use rushes much, in the short days . . . but the very poor—who are always the worst economists and therefore must continue very poor—buy a halfpenny candle every evening, which in their blowing open rooms, does not burn for much more than two hours." The incentive to thrift was too often lacking. "I never knew one instance," writes Young, "of any poor man's working diligently while young and in health to escape coming to the parish when ill or old." It may be doubted whether his utmost efforts could have achieved such an object. But the prospect of being able to take a small farm was a far more potent incentive to industry. The great social loss of enclosures was that they broke the ladder by which the labourer could get, with luck, first a cottage with grazing rights, and then a small farm.

The enclosure of commons meant a loss to the poorer villagers for which it would have been difficult to make any adequate compensation. A small piece of land without rights of common, or a lump sum, even if a fair money equivalent, was comparatively valueless. And there were many who used the common on sufference, or who got no compensation because the rights were attached to cottages of which they were tenants only. An impartial enclosure commissioner reported, "Numbers in the practice of feeding on the commons cannot prove their rights; and many, indeed most, who have allotments have not more than an acre, which being insufficient for the man's cow, both cow and land are sold to the opulent farmer." Here again is the raw material of many tragedies.

Then there were squatters on commons who had been there on suffrance in huts they had built for themselves. Many were simply evicted. Some people spoke as if these were all industrious peasants, some as if they were all marauding vagabonds. The fact is, both classes existed. To Bacon, in the early seventeenth century, all cottagers had been "housed beggars." King, at the end of the century, had computed that one fifth of 500,000 cottage families (not only, be it noted, the squatters on heaths) might be able to earn a subsistence without poor relief or charity.[1]

[1] See above, p. 12.

In the later eighteenth century much is heard of the industrious cottager who works as a day labourer while his wife looks after pigs and cows. It is not to be doubted that the cottager had shared in the increased wealth of the country. But commons were still the natural resort of poor and idle people. Wordsworth writes of the "race of beggars," "abject and degraded," who inhabit the "crazy huts" and "tottering hovels" on commons:

> Such on the breast of darksome heaths are found;
> And with their parents occupy the skirts
> Of furze-clad commons.

Similar descriptions of the dwellers on commons had been made for the past two centuries. One old writer describes the cattle on commons as like the men, "a starved, scabby and rascally race." And squatters on commons had long been resented by the legal commoners whose rights they infringed. The unfortunate "Act for the settlement of the Poor" of 1662 had been passed, so its preamble recited, because "poor people . . . do endeavour to settle themselves in those parishes where there is the best stock, the largest commons or wastes to build cottages, and the most wood for them to burn and destroy."

With all these accounts of the genus cottager it is interesting to get a glimpse of an actual family of squatters, the victim of the resentment of those with common rights. It is described by William Hutton, who in 1750 lost his way and was benighted in crossing Charnwood Forest, five miles of uncultivated waste without a road. At last he found a building of some sort and induced its unwilling occupant to give him shelter. The man (in the dark) appeared tall and strong-built, but "his manner was repelling as the rain, and his appearance horrid as the night." Next morning he was revealed as "formed in one of Nature's largest and coarsest moulds. His hands retained the accumulated filth of the last three months, garnished with half a dozen scabs; both, perhaps, the result of idleness." His wife was "young, handsome, ragged and good-natured." Three children and a hideous aunt made up the household which represented for Hutton the most complete poverty and the most extreme idleness he had ever encountered. Both were partly at least due to "a mob of freeholders" who had destroyed all the man's outbuildings and so (presumably) prevented him from keeping beasts to graze upon the common. They had no candle, no fire beyond "a glow which would barely have roasted a potato." This truly hospitable family told him "we have no eatables whatever, except some pease porridge, which is rather thin, only pease and water, and which we are ashamed to offer." For bedclothes Hutton was given the wife's petticoat: "she robbed her bed to supply mine."

It was argued that enclosures would not only enormously increase the productiveness of the land, but would eliminate much idleness and even crime. Doubtless in some cases they did, but then they also brought poverty and idleness of another kind. Young himself, a whole-hearted advocate of enclosures and the economy of the large farm, came to realize this. After the terrible year 1800, when corn prices reached the highest level ever known in England, he wrote (in 1801), "Go to an ale-house kitchen of an old-enclosed country, and there you will see the origin of poverty and high poor-rates. For whom are they to be sober? For whom are they to save? (Such are their questions.) For the parish? If I am diligent, shall I have leave to build a cottage? If I am sober, shall I have land for a cow? If I am frugal, shall I have half an acre of potatoes? You offer no motives;

you have nothing but a parish officer and a workhouse!—Bring me another pot."

Against this may be set his other pronouncement (in 1775): "It may be laid down as a maxim, that without inclosures there can be no good husbandry: while a county is laid out in open fields, every farmer tied down to the husbandry of his slovenly neighbour, there can be no good husbandry." The dilemma might perhaps have been escaped—in some places it was so escaped—if more regard had been had for the claims, moral as well as legal, of cottagers and the poor. But this course too had its dangers: the more uninstructed and public-spirited of the advocates of enclosure and the large farm, notably Sir John Sinclair and Arthur Young, were conscious of the evils of over-subdivision of land which were manifest in Ireland and parts of France. A striking passage by Young, the outcome of his tour in France, deserves more attention than it has been given. "I would prohibit the division of small farms, which is as mischievous to cultivation as it is sure to be distressing to the people. If you would see a district, with as little distress in it as is consistent with the political system of the old government of France, you must assuredly go where there are no little properties at all . . . and if in such districts you should, contrary to this rule, meet with much distress, it is twenty to one but that it is a parish which has some commons that tempt the poor people to have some cattle, to have property, and in consequence misery. When you are engaged in this political tour, finish it by seeing England, and I will show you a set of peasants well clothed, well nourished, tolerably drunken from superfluity, well lodged and at their ease ; and yet amongst them, not one in a thousand has either land or cattle. When you have viewed all this, go back to your tribune, and preach, if you please, in favour of a minute division of landed property." Yet this same Arthur Young, on this same tour whose lessons he is here evaluating, coined the famous phrase "the magic of property turns sand into gold."

The class of large, rich and enterprising farmers who were the outcome of the new agriculture roused much dislike. They were not without precedent—Baxter noted that there were rich farmers round London who would be considered in other parts of the country as gentlemen of great estate. But in the later eighteenth century they were regarded as new rich and as a cause instead of a result of high prices. They had new-fangled ways; they aped the manners of the gentry; their wives and daughters were accused of being too fine to attend to the dairy. The multiplication of this class had the unfortunate effect of widening the gulf between the labourer and the farmer. The dislike they provoked has been most eloquently voiced by Cobbett. But Cobbett was a large farmer himself, and (when he is being practical, not political) he extols the methods possible only to the large farmer. Crabbe, who set himself against the sentimentality which idealized the peasant's lot :

> ('I paint the Cot,
> As Truth will paint it, and as Bards will not.')

draws a striking contrast between the farmer's household, old and new. The modern farmer's wife has learnt the accomplishments so much decried :

> And though the bride, now free from school, admits
> Of pride implanted there, some transient fits;
> Yet soon she casts her girlish flights aside,
> And in substantial blessings rests her pride.
> No more she moves in measured steps; no more
> Runs, with bewilder'd ear, her music o'er;
> No more recites her French the hinds among,

But chides her maidens in her mother-tongue ;
Her tambour-frame she leaves and diet spare,
Plain work and plenty with her house to share ;
Till, all her varnish lost in few short years,
In all her worth the farmer's wife appears.
Yet not the ancient kind ; nor she who gave
Her soul to gain—a mistress and a slave :
Who, not to sleep allow'd the needful time ;
To whom repose was loss, and sport a crime :
Who, in her meanest room (and all were mean)
A noisy drudge, from morn till night was seen ;
But she, the daughter, boasts a decent room
Adorned with carpet, formed in Wilton's loom ;
Fair prints along the paper'd walls are spread ;
There, Werther sees the sportive children fed,
And Charlotte, here, bewails her lover dead.[1]

One may have a sentimental regret for the old broadside ballads which had been pasted on the rough plastered walls of farms and cottages, and which clearly had no place along these "paper'd walls," but contemporaries denounced the carpets and furniture of the well-furnished farm-house as if they had been signs of depravity.

The new-fangled farmer, who was a farmer's son, had often received a farming education by being boarded-out as a pupil with an improving farmer. And "a regular school education" for the first

[1] *The Parish Register*, 1807

time was not given solely so that the son of a farmer might enter a trade or profession.[1]

Another result of agricultural enthusiasm and village reorganization was an improvement in rural housing. For two reasons there had been a constant war on cottages in many villages. One to keep down the rates, the other because the farmers disliked cottages near commons as they regarded pasturing the cottagers' beasts as an infringement of their rights of common. For this reason many cottages had been razed to the ground on the pretext that they harboured thieves. Indeed the policy of preventing cottage-building had the sanction of the Act of Elizabeth "Against the creating and maintaining of cottages," and under that Act (repealed in 1775) no cottage might be built without the leave of Quarter Sessions, with certain exceptions—notably the parish cottage on the waste to house the impotent poor. The result was terrible overcrowding. To quote Arthur Young (in 1773): "Cottages are in general the habitation of labourers, who all swarm with children, and many have double, treble, and even quadruple

[1] W. Marshall, *The Rural Economy of the Midland Counties*, 1790, i, 115 ff.

families. And in most parishes view the parish cottages with dozens of families in them." [1]

With enclosure one motive for the destruction of cottages disappeared. New farmhouses were built on the compact farms, and the old ones which had all been crowded together in the village were divided into cottages for labourers. Some miserable shacks on commons disappeared. For the first time cottage-building attracted the attention of architects; plans were published; improving landlords made it a point of pride or honour to build decent cottages, and the state of cottages became an object of enquiry with the Board of Agriculture. Plans and specifications were published and landowners urged to remedy a state of things in which "half the poor" were forced to live in "shattered hovels." "Humanity shudders," said the steward of the Marquis of Bath (in an *Address to the Landowners of this Kingdom; with Plans of Cottages*), "at the idea of the industrious labourer, with a wife and five or six children, being obliged to live, or rather to exist, in a wretched, damp, gloomy room, of ten or twelve feet square, and that room without a floor; but common decency must revolt at considering, that

[1] *Northern Tour*, iv, 416.

over this wretched apartment there is only *one* chamber, to hold all the miserable beds of the miserable family." In Wales, as in Scotland, and the more backward parts of the country, housing was conspicuously worse.[1]

Possibly the cottage-building landlord was not very common, still agricultural improvement was by no means entirely detrimental to "the labouring poor." "Let us look below the inhabitants of the middle classes," wrote Jonas Hanway in 1784, "we find their cottages better and larger, their food and raiment superior in quality to what it was, and most things in an improving condition."

Disaster fell upon the village at the end of the century, and things became worse with the hard times which followed the peace. Prices in the bad years rose faster than wages and fluctuated violently. The employment of women and children began to dwindle as spinning became a machine industry. Many labourers had lost the cows which had been their stand-by in bad times. In 1795 a bad harvest sent bread up to famine prices. Some Berkshire magistrates, meeting in quarter sessions

[1] G. E. Fussell and C. Goodman, *The housing of the rural population in the eighteenth century.* "Econ. Journal. History Supplement," Jan. 1930

at Speenhamland, agreed to solve the problem, not by recommending a rise in wages which the farmers could well have afforded, but by ordering an allowance in aid of wages to be paid out of the poor-rates in proportion to the price of bread and the size of the family. They published a table known as "the bread scales," which was widely adopted. Thus a device, purely local in its origin and intended to meet an emergency, became general and stereotyped. The effects were calamitous, but they were not fully felt till peace brought bad times. They were particularly disastrous to the small farmer who employed little or no labour, but shared in the poor-rates swollen by the rate in aid of wages. Wages fell, the "man on the rates" especially if he had many children, was in a much better position than the independent labourer, who could not compete with the rate-aided labour which the farmers preferred.

A dreadful state of demoralization followed, where the rate in aid of wages prevailed, which was not everywhere—the north was more or less free from the blight. It was found that the possession of an allotment or a cow was a barrier against this pauperization, and it was realized that the depriving the labourer of his rights of common had been a calamity. A movement for allotments began in a very small way which was the germ of the present movement for small-holdings, though for many years nothing much was done.

Thus a combination of evils fell upon the village: loss of commons, loss of by-industries, pauperization by a demoralizing poor law. Yet all this needs qualification. Loss of commons was a local not a general calamity, and enclosure was not invariably harmful to the labourer. The introduction of the potato, in spite of Cobbett, was a real benefit to farmer and labourer alike, since the English labourer, unlike the Irish peasant, was never reduced to the potato standard.[1] If spinning declined, there were places where other by-industries increased, notably straw-plaiting, which flourished exceedingly during the war, when the supply of Italian straw hats was cut off. The rate in aid of wages was not new, but it was given in a far more wholesale way, and this demoralizing liberality was probably a contributing cause to the remarkable decline in the death-

[1] See p. 158. The cultivation of potatoes in Lancashire was commented on in 1774: the farmer "often depends more upon a good crop of potatoes than of wheat or any other grain," the potato being "an article highly useful to the poor, acceptable to the rich and profitable to the industrious farmer." *London Magazine*, 1774, p. 238.

rate between 1780 and 1820.[1] A flood of light was directed on the village by the enclosure controversy and by the new spirit of social enquiry and humanitarianism. The same instinct to idealize the past which made weavers and framework knitters look back to a golden age, which had existed, if at all, only for short times and in exceptional cases, is seen in pictures of village life which are contradicted by every attempt to investigate actual conditions. Rural prosperity was based on the labour of women and children. Low food prices had been based on the over-production of corn and on the poverty of the small farmer who sold in the worst markets the pigs and chickens and butter he could not afford to eat. The blight of a scandalously administered poor law had lain on the village, at least since 1662. In the purely agricultural districts, according to Defoe, in 1728, the children as they grew up were apt to run

[1] Rickman, who was responsible for the census, wrote to d'Ivernois in 1827, " It is not for Mr. Rickman to assign causes for the decrease of mortality ; if he might venture further than in the Preliminary Observations to the Census of 1811 and 1821 . . . he would ascribe it to the general use of tea and sugar, and to the increased operation of the Poor Relief Laws, which ensure wholesome food and medical attendance to all. But these arguments would encounter contradiction in England." *Minutes of Evidence, Population Bill Committee*, 1830.

away to be footmen and soldiers, thieves and beggars, or sell themselves to the plantations to avoid the gaol and the gallows. It was assumed that every married labourer was likely to be a burden on the rates. In illness and old age the parish was almost inevitably his only resort. Crabbe's "noble peasant," Isaac Ashford—had only one dread; the inevitable workhouse in old age, from which he was mercifully delivered by sudden death at his cottage gate. The poor man's way of making provision for his old age was to establish a right to a settlement, and with this end apprenticeships were entered into and even farms rented.

Status depended largely on the poor law. There was a gulf between the farmers, who held, generally in rotation, the office of parish overseer, and whose chief object was to keep down the rates (except in so far as they could exploit them for their own purposes), and the labourers, who were classed as "the poor."

The devices used to prevent people obtaining a settlement in a parish, and so a right to relief, beggar description. One was to destroy cottages lest they should become the nest of "beggars' brats." The hustling of pregnant women out of parishes lest the expected child should gain a settlement was done with the most callous brutality. Here is an entry from the records of a Cambridgeshire parish : Seventeen and sixpence was paid to remove " Mary Pateman neear her labour and suspected alsoe to be sick of the small poc. To send her away with all convenient speed and in time." And there are worse entries than this.

Couples were forced to marry under threats of penalties under the bastardy laws so that the woman and her child should be burdens upon some other parish. Such was the marriage which Parson Woodforde recorded in his diary on November 22, 1769 : " I married Tom Bunge of Amsford to Charity Andrews of Castle Cary by License this morning. The Parish of Cary made him marry her, and he came handcuffed to Church for fear of running away, and the Parish of Cary was at all the expence of bringing them to, I received of Mr. Andrew Russ the Overseer of the Parish of Cary for it .0. 10. 6."

The parish poor-house was usually a place of horror, some ruinous cottage into which those of all ages, sick or well, were crammed. Crabbe's description is well known. Yet an undoubted claim on such a place was an object of supreme importance to the labourer. The riots in East Anglia in 1765 against the building of large work-houses to serve a number of parishes and supersede the wretched parish poor-houses speak for themselves. The House of Industry, as it was called, on Nacton Heath was threatened by a mob of about four hundred labourers. When the magistrates tried to persuade them to disperse they answered that they came to fight for their liberties. They were resolved the poor should be maintained in their own parishes, they might as well die there as be starved and they were determined to pull down the house. However a few soldiers from Ipswich, and the reading of the Riot Act, dispersed them without serious casualties. Ten days later there was a similar attack on a house which was being built at Bulcamp.

There had been a serious drought, and the first day the mob said " God would not suffer it to rain till Bulcamp Hell was pulled down."

Next day it did rain, and the rioters were confirmed in their purpose; the building, what there was of it, was demolished.

When threatened with troops, they said, " If the king was to send 1000 soldiers it would give them no concern, for they could raise 10,000 and did not fear defeating the soldiers."[1] Only a very personal interest in the place could have impelled them to such violence.

The evils which were revealed by the stress of hard times had long existed. They had been mitigated by access to commons for fuel and pasture and by by-industries—in some places, but not in all. And both these things had tended to keep wages low and had depended on the work of women and children. The position of the labourer was fundamentally unsound. He was victimized by a poor-law administration which was at first—with exceptions of course—harshly deterrent, and then exactly the reverse. The farmers then discovered a way of shuffling part of their wages-bill on to the rates with disastrous consequences.

[1] *State Papers Domestic* ,1765, P.R.O.

CHAPTER VI

THE COMING OF INDUSTRIALISM

THE term " Industrial Revolution " has been a little disparaged lately by historians. When using it, it is prudent to add the qualifying " so-called." And though it would clearly be impossible to overrate the coming of industrialism which has transformed the country and moulded the lives of its inhabitants, we know now that the changes were gradual—they had been coming for centuries. Evolution, perhaps, would be a better word than revolution. It is quite impossible to take a date, say 1760, and say ' here begins the Industrial Revolution '—and equally unsound to make it end somewhere about 1830 or even 1850. The process of industrialization began before the eighteenth century and has been going on at an increasing rate ever since. And why industrial, it is even asked, since it is impossible to separate changes in industry from changes in population, in transport, in agriculture, and in social structure. Each acted and reacted on the other. Again, though the interrelation is less direct, the changes in the spirit of the age and in literary fashion—the new humanitarianism, sentimentalism, romanticism, the cult of the noble savage—are all connected with the growth of an urban civilization and the increasing command over nature.

But when all this is said, the years between 1760 and 1830 were critical years, and the familiar account of the transformation is sound in its selection of three essential factors: First, inventions in textile machinery leading to a great expansion in the cotton industry. Secondly, developments in the iron industry based on the smelting of iron with coal instead of charcoal. Thirdly, the improvement of the steam-engine. These things led to the age of the machine, the factory and the industrial town. The population massed itself in the coal and iron districts, towns grew hideously, and England became an industrial instead of a mainly agricultural country. By 1815, or even 1830, the process had not gone very far.

But the inventions of Hargreaves, and Crompton and Watt and the others were not a first cause. Why was there this outbreak of invention, and why did it take the particular form it did? In the past, inventors had spent their lives in searching for the secret of perpetual motion, or for the elixir of life. Now attention is concentrated on the definite needs of industry. Why was this?

Since the beginning of the century there had been a great advance, both in trade and industry—that of trade was relatively more conspicuous in the early part of the century: Liverpool, the port, increased its population tenfold from 1680 to 1760; Manchester, the manufacturing town, multiplied its population by five between 1717 and 1773. The banking system was developing rapidly and the banks mobilized capital and put it at the service of industry. Industry was already capitalized and organized for foreign trade. The domestic weaver was one link in a chain of persons and interests by which the wool from the sheep's back was exported in the form of cloth. Domestic industry and the small producer were dependent for their raw material on highly organized capitalistic concerns. For instance, large companies produced copper and brass ingots which the small working brass founders or braziers of Birmingham and London worked up. Large furnaces and forges supplied the domestic cutlers of Sheffield with their raw material; the nailers at their little country smithies made nails from the rods produced in large slitting mills; a chain of middlemen and merchants organized the collection and distribution of their products for inland trade and export.

Capitalism was the cause of the industrial revolution rather than its result. On the other hand, the industrial inventions were a result of industrial advance rather than its cause, though of course they meant further strides forward. Even in the early part of the century there was a belief in the advantage of a division of labour and of labour-saving machines. Le Blanc, a French visitor in the forties, was much impressed with the advance already made in this direction. "England," he writes, "has more than any other of those machines which really multiply men by lessening their work, and by means of which one man can execute what would take up thirty without their assistance." He instances Newcomen's steam-engine and the sort of simple machine or tool used for mass production in the Birmingham toy trade (as well as for the minting of coins) by which such things as snuff-boxes, buckles and heads for canes were stamped out and polished.

"Thus by turning a wheel,[1] a boy of ten years old gives to a hundred things made of steel, all at the same time, that beautiful polish, which few of our French workmen can imitate."

Till recently England had been an imitator rather than an innovator. For instance, the new husbandry with its root crops was Dutch. French refugees had brought new methods of silk-weaving and paper-making. The new silk-throwing or twisting machinery was Italian. England had to her credit the stocking-frame, which had thrown out of work many hand-knitters of stockings but had laid the foundations of the hosiery industry, and the use of the steam-engine for pumping. And—a most important thing—in scientific craftmanship, such as watch-making and the making of mathematical instruments, she was supreme. Hence one great source of the inventors and mechanics who made and improved the new machines. The fully fledged textile factory had existed since about 1719. This was Lombe's famous silk-mill at Derby. It is particularly interesting because it was the model for Arkwright's cotton-spinning factories and thus the prototype of the Lancashire cotton-mill of the

[1] Compare below, p. 203.

nineteenth century, except that it had a large water-wheel instead of tall chimneys. It was a huge five-storied stone-built block with 468 windows and was one of the sights of the country. Successive generations of visitors described with admiration the complicated machinery which yet made the process of twisting and winding the silk so simple that it was chiefly done by women and children. A legend grew up about the way in which Lombe's brother had procured the secret of the machinery from Italy at the cost of his life, and when Sir Thomas Lombe died he was reputed to have been poisoned by angry Italians. When, in 1732, Parliament—at the request of other manufacturers—refused to extend Lombe's patent, silk-mills multiplied in Macclesfield, Congleton and elsewhere. By the middle of the century the factory system was actually in being, but since silk was a comparatively small industry it made little mark on the country. And since no one had yet dreamed that the employment of women and children was other than highly beneficent to Society, no one had complained that few of the factory hands were men.

Though by the forties trade and industry were in a flourishing condition, there were some gloomy spots. Transport though improving was still very bad. The production of iron was in a decaying state, though the industries which used iron in Birmingham and Sheffield and elsewhere were growing. The difficulty was that of fuel: the output of English forges was shrinking; imports of iron from Sweden, Russia, America, increased, but were liable to interruption by war. It was well known that the remedy lay in the discovery of effective processes for smelting and refining iron with coal or coke instead of charcoal. This was achieved by the inventions of the two Darbys of Coalbrookdale and, later, of Cort. The foundries, instead of seeking wood and water, which had induced them to migrate from Sussex to Shropshire, established themselves in the coal and iron districts. The production of iron increased enormously, and the age of the machine became possible.

These discoveries triumphantly reversed the situation so far as iron was concerned. Another felt want was something which would increase the productiveness of the spinning wheel. After the invention of Kay's flying shuttle weavers were constantly at a stand for want of yarn. There had long been also a much-desired thing, and that was the establishment of some industry which would employ the unemployed and the unemployable, and more particularly women and children. The desire was achieved in a way which reminds one of those stories where a wish is fulfilled by some malignant being and the fulfilment brings tragedy. For generations people had been saying that the creation of a linen industry would " set the poor on work " as the phrase went. And it had long been deplored that England had no manufacture which could compete with French cambrics and Dutch lawns.[1] For instance, one old writer had said that the making of linen would be " an employment for the weakest people, not capable of stronger work, being widows and aged and decrepit people, now the most chargeable, likewise for beggars and vagrants, who now live idly and by the sweat of other men's labours." Linen did not materialise to any purpose, but cotton did.

The inventions of Hargreaves and Crompton and the others created what was in effect a new industry. Its rapid and dramatic growth seemed like a miracle, particularly the making of muslin, which the fine, strong thread spun by the mule

[1] See above, p. 49.

made possible. The new fabrics could and did compete with India muslins, Holland lawns and French cambrics. The wearing of the new fresh-looking cottons seemed a symbol of progress. An observer remarked (1795) that muslin-clad daughters succeeded to mothers dressed in linsey-woolsey, a change even more striking than that in our day from worsted to "art-silk" stockings. For the new cottons Francis Place tells us worked "all but wonders in the health and cleanliness of women." Dress went through something like the revolution which has transformed it since the war. The poorer classes discarded the petticoats quilted with horsehair and the leather stays "worn till they dropped to pieces from dirt."

The result of this enormous expansion of cotton-spinning was, first, the golden age of the domestic weaver, when, as Radcliffe says, "We employed every person in cotton weaving who could be induced to learn the trade, but want of population, want of hands, and want of looms, set us fast." Bamford knew a soldier who came home on furlough during the war, sat down to the loom, got his leave extended, and earned enough money to buy his discharge from the Army. Calico-weaving was easily learnt, men, women and children flocked to the loom. The status of the domestic weaver, like his wages, was brought down by an influx of agricultural labourers and others, English, Welsh and Irish with very low standards of living. Muslin weaving was a more difficult art and the muslin weavers of Bolton (so it is said) refused to admit the " common journeymen " of other trades to the public-houses they patronized, dressed like the middle class, swaggered about swinging their canes, and were even said to stick five-pound notes in the hatbands of their hats. These people and their children were the hand-loom weavers whose sufferings in competition with themselves and with the power-loom were to be so long-drawn-out.

Each generation sees the Industrial Revolution from a different standpoint. Indeed, it has so many aspects, its manifestations at different times and in different places have varied so much that by the judicious selection of facts it is easy to represent it in very conflicting ways.

Modern historians have shown how slow was the coming of the machine and the factory, and have stressed the fact that the so-called revolution in the eighteenth century was almost confined to cotton and iron ; that the date of an invention and its effective use in industry are two very different things; that in 1830 the great majority of workers were still outside the factory system; that some of the evils of transition—and notably the misfortunes of the hand-loom weavers—were increased because the new methods took so long to establish themselves.[1] By tracing back origins on one hand, and by correcting false notions of the great rapidity of the change on the other, they have corrected the over-insistence on those critical years, so dear to text-books, between 1760 and 1830. But there is no doubt at all that the time did seem epoch-making to those who lived in it, and in fact was epoch-making.

One might suppose the term revolution as applied to industrial change would have been suggested by the French Revolution. And so it was. Blanqui, the French economist, is said to have been the first to speak of the industrial revolution in the early nineteenth century, to show that he thought economic change in England as revolutionary as political change in France, France had had a political revolution, England an economic one. The idea was developed by Marx but the term did not come into general use till Toynbee used it in lectures given in 1881 which were pub-

[1] Cf. J. H. Clapham, *An Economic History of Modern Britain*, 1926.

lished as *The Industrial Revolution of the Eighteenth Century in England.*

But before events in France had suggested the analogy, people were fond of saying that there had been a revolution in this or that industry. There was an exhilarating sense of a growing command over Nature, and of vast possibilities of capturing the markets of the world. The inventions had supplied the country's needs so dramatically that it seemed as if Providence had concerned itself to make England the workshop of the world. The inventions came of course as the answer to repeated experiment, directed to definite ends, but achievement surpassed expectation. While the Society of Arts in the fifties offered prizes for a machine which would spin six threads at once, the jenny, after improvements, could spin a hundred; while the mule and the water-frame were yet more marvellous. The magazines paid great attention to new machines and processes and the Press as a whole was eloquent and high-flown. It worked to death the epithets 'incredible,' 'unexampled,' 'amazing,' 'unparalleled,' and the like. As early as 1767 an enthusiast said of improved roads and the first canals, "there never was a more astonishing revolution than this." The sober *Encyclopædia*

Britannica averred that " the discoveries and improvements " of the age " diffuse a glory over this country unattainable by conquest or dominion." In 1784 it was said, alas, optimistically, that the new discoveries " give the command of the iron trade of the world to Great Britain, and take it for ever, or at least so long as the industry and liberty of Britain remain, from the northern countries and from America, because Britain is the only country hitherto known in which seams of coal . . . iron ore and lime-stone . . . are frequently found in the same fields and in the neighbourhood of the sea."

The writer had not visualized the possibilities of steam, but these had particularly captured the imagination of his contemporaries. When Boswell, that prince of interviewers, visited Soho in 1776, where Boulton and Watt were constructing their steam-engines, Boulton, whom he calls the iron chieftain, said to him, " I sell here what all the world desires, power." In 1784 the first balloon ascent was made in England, when Lunardi, secretary to the Neapolitan ambassador, was, as he says, " the first aerial traveller in the English atmosphere." He went up, amidst immense excitement, with a cat as passenger, from the

T. Deeble, Sculp.

View of the ascent of Mr. Lunardi's celebrated Air Balloon from the Artillery Ground, September 15th, 1784

[*face p.* 154

Artillery Garden (close to Bedlam, as sceptics pointed out), landed the cat—which had suffered from the cold—at South Mimms, and finally descended in a cornfield at Ware in Hertfordshire. Men's minds began to dwell on the possibilities of steam and aerial navigation. Erasmus Darwin, in 1792, described, with unpoetic precision, the actual achievements of steam :

> The giant-Power from earth's remotest caves
> Lifts with strong arm her dark reluctant waves :
> Here high in air the rising stream he pours
> To clay built cisterns, or to lead-lined towers :
> Fresh thro' a thousand pipes the wave distils,
> And thirsty cities drink the exuberant rills.
> There the vast mill-stone with inebriate whirl
> On trembling floors his forceful fingers twirl,
> Feast without blood ! and nourish human-kind.

It may be as well to explain that these lines refer to the pumping of water from coal-mines for drainage and from rivers for the purposes of water-supply—this last was done in London from the Thames. Then comes an evident allusion to the Albion mills built in London by Watt in 1786, with the help of Rennie. Fifty pairs of mill-stones were set in motion by two engines. It created a sensation and it became the fashion to visit it—to Watt's annoyance: "What have Dukes, Lords and Ladies to do with masquerading in a flour mill?" he wrote to Boulton.

Darwin then went on to prophesy:

Soon shall thy arm, UNCONQUER'D STEAM! afar
Drag the slow barge, or drive the rapid car;
Or on wide-waving wings expanded bear
The flying-chariot through the fields of air.
Fair crews triumphant, leaning from above,
Shall wave their fluttering kerchiefs as they move;
Or warrior-bands alarm the gaping crowd,
And armies shrink beneath the shadowy cloud.

During the eighteenth century it was the beneficent rather than the catastrophic aspects of the changes which captured attention.

We know how cotton and iron enabled England to resist Napoleon and subsidize her allies. But what is often forgotten is the marvellous way in which the growth of industry and trade mitigated disaster during the American War (1775–83) and was the basis of the wonderful recovery which the country made during the ten years' peace which followed. As a recent historian has said, "there can be few if any cases of national recovery on record so swift or so complete as this." [1]

[1] R. Coupland, *The American Revolution and the British Empire*, 1930, 46–7.

And first for a survey of trade in the first year of the war, which was sent, by one Charles Irving, to the office of the Colonial Secretary: "To begin with Warwickshire, I found that the exports of Birmingham ware in all the different branches are just now considerably greater than has ever been known in any former period. In the adjacent places and in this County and in Staffordshire the Nail trade seems less brisk than formerly; but any spare Hands from that Branch find full Employment in other hardware manufactories. Derbyshire is at present much more flourishing in the silk throwster way and in the manufactory of woollen stockings than formerly; which is evident from the number of Machines lately erected in both these Branches. The fine Pottery manufacture in Derby is also greatly increased. In Lancashire the Manchester cotton manufactories are in the most flourishing situation. The improvement in their cut velvets, velverets, and other goods has opened to them a market even at Naples, Messina, and other parts of the Mediterranean, which is perhaps not only owing to their cheapness, but likewise to an improvement they have lately made in their taste of Paterns. In Yorkshire, particularly in Halifax, Bradford and Leeds, the coarse cloth manufacture was never known in a better state, or a greater number of Hands employed, and more extensive schemes projected for advancing it still further. At Leeds likewise the Potters work so highly improved both in composition and elegance of figure as to make it an object of considerable export. At Whitby the building of Ships and making of Sail cloth continue to be as extensive as formerly; and at Hull a greater tonage of Shipping is just now employed than ever was known; which no doubt is greatly occasioned by the vigorous state of the manufactories of Lancashire as well as in the different parts of Yorkshire chiefly shipped from this Port.

"From the observations I have made of the state of the manufactories in general, I am induced to think that the present flourishing condition is not a little owing to the two following causes, viz.: first, the great improvements in Machinery, by which the expense of labour is much diminished and the perfection of the work increased; secondly, the cheapness of fuel, which is more universally diffused by means of internal navigation and the more easy communication by land, to which may be added the universal practice of cultivating potatoes which are experimentally found to be the cheapest of all food. These causes make the manufacturers to sell their commodities at a cheaper rate, while at the same time the degree of perfection [to] which their several branches are now brought, open to them a ready market in most parts of Europe; an advantage to this country which I apprehend will continue to increase; for although the wages of manufacturers in foreign countries are lower than here, yet the benefit arising from the large stock employed in trade in England, with the great improvement in machinery, and the plenty of fuel so absolutely necessary in most of the manufactories, do much more than counterbalance that circumstance. To this great consumption of our commodities on the Continent, I presume it is owing that the interruptions of commerce with America has been little felt." [1]

Warwickshire and Birmingham are already remarkable for the 'economic resiliency' which has been so characteristic of their history since 1860.[2] This is the more noteworthy since the apprenticeship laws, so far as they were effective, prevented the transference of labour from one

[1] MSS. letter, Sept. 28, 1775. P.R.O. *Colonial Office*, 5/154, No. 188.

[2] G. C. Allen, *The Industrial Development of Birmingham and the Black Country*, 1860–1927, 1929.

with their acquired skill made valueless. And the suffering was made greater by the sense of being excluded from the benefits of an enormous increase of wealth.

The sense of the catastrophic nature of the revolution was hardly expressed before the thirties and was then connected with the enquiries into conditions in the factories. Still, the fact that a social revolution was in progress had been noticed here and there. The changes were most startling in Lancashire, and attracted the attention of Whitaker, parson and topographer, when he investigated the origins of wealthy and landed families in Whalley : " Those opulent houses whose property is not to be traced to a feudal origin, have been generally raised by the profession of the law. Some indeed have grown to consequence by habits of economy and gradual accumulation. But a new principle is now introduced, which threatens gradually to absorb the whole property of the district within its vortex. I mean the principle of manufactures, aided by the two dangerous sciences of Chemistry and Mechanics. The operation of this principle is accompanied with another effect, of which it is impossible to speak, but in the language at once of sorrow and indignation.

Indeed, it can only be considered so much pure unmixed evil, moral, medical, religious and political. In great manufactories, human corruption, accumulated in large masses, seems to undergo a kind of fermentation, which sublimes it to a degree of malignity not to be exceeded out of Hell." But Whitaker was no blind admirer of rural simplicity. His description of Lancashire in the process of its great transformation deserves quotation: Before the coming of manufactures "society languished by dispersion. . . . In those parts of the district before us, of which the population is scattered in inconsiderable villages, civilization is in a very backward state. Farmers and husbandmen are, of all mankind, least impressible with the truths of religion—selfish, fraudulent, competing, intemperate, with rigid nerves and firm health. . . ." This is almost the attitude of a modern novelist towards village life and far removed from the sentimental idealism of the eighteenth century.

After his condemnation of manufactures, it is strange to find he considers that "on the whole society had greatly the advantage" in manufacturing towns and districts, where if there is more fanaticism (i.e. dissent) there is more religion (owing to the weak health and sedentary habits of artisans), a better police—and "charity more liberally and systematically administered."[1]

Marx, in the forties, accepting the views of the early English socialists, saw in the recent advance in industrialization the beginning of a capitalistic age, the cause of a growth of capital. But though capital was enormously increased, the revolution was rather a result of the capitalization of trade and industry which had gone far under the so-called domestic system.

To Toynbee, who wrote when the doctrines of *laissez-faire* were being attacked on all sides, the essence of the revolution was "the substitution of competition for the medieval regulations which had controlled the production and distribution of wealth." But, though of course competition was enormously increased, the old regulations were already obsolete or in decay. The new regulations, the chief of course being the Factory Acts, began in a very small way with the turn of the century and were the direct result of the new methods.

In this generation one would expect a disposition to stress the effects of war on the industrial revolution. These were certainly very great and (before

[1] T. D. Whitaker, *History of the original Parish of Whalley*, 1801, pp. 482–3.

1914) had been unduly neglected. It is scarcely possible to distinguish them from the effects of economic change. For nearly a quarter of a century industry and trade had been dominated by war conditions and a war mentality. The change over to peace was catastrophic. War had produced political reaction which had poisoned relations between masters and men and embittered industrial change. It is difficult to distinguish between the effects of machinery, of a demoralizing poor-law, of unsound finance and a burden of debt, of a devastating torrent of Irish labour, of an obsolete system of central and local government, of the sudden cessation of employment directly dependent on war. And it is still more difficult to imagine what the post-war years would have been like without the expansion of production due to the new inventions.

CHAPTER VII

CHILD LABOUR AND APPRENTICESHIP

OF all the revolutions of an age of revolutions none was more complete than that revealed by the attitude towards child-labour in cotton-mills. That children should be inured to labour at the earliest possible age had long been a social ideal. To Defoe on his tour through England, the chief criterion of prosperity had been the extent of the employment of young children. "Hardly any thing above four years old but its hands are sufficient to itself," he wrote enthusiastically of Halifax. Round Norwich, "the very children after four or five years of age, could every one earn their own bread." Industrialists and manufacturers had long appealed to Parliament for special favours on the grounds of the number of women and children whom they employed. Here, for instance, is a plea for that pampered industry, the woollen manufacture: "The poor people take their children from the highways and from their infant idleness, and bring them to wool and wheel." The spinning school had anticipated the factory, indeed it had been an embryo factory where each child sat at its spinning wheel. Locke, in 1697, had urged that all poor children above the age of three should be taught to earn their living at working schools for spinning and knitting. And nearly a century later David Davies, a country clergyman whose attitude to the poor was undeniably sympathetic, recommended that no poor relief should be given on behalf of any child over six who could not knit, or of any child over nine who could not spin linen or wool.

Generations of visitors had admired the Derby silk-mill where the work was chiefly done by women and children. Other embryo factories had been similarly admired. For instance, Curwen, an American loyalist, visiting Halifax in 1777, watched some fifteen children making wire cards for wool-carding, "which employment" he noted in his diary, "not only keeps their little minds from vice but . . . takes a heavy burden from their poor parents." That was the traditional and unquestioned attitude towards the labour of children.

Child labour in those days was generally under-

behave badly, when the indentures would be cancelled: the master would keep the fee and begin again with a new boy and another fee. It goes without saying that the poorer and the more friendless, the more liable the apprentice was to ill-treatment. Semi-starvation was the lot of many apprentices who were not otherwise ill-treated.

Apprenticeship meant very different things for the comparatively well-to-do and for the poor. For the first it meant admission to an exclusive craft or business in return for a premium. Where conditions of board and lodging were good, and where the trade was an eligible one, a correspondingly large fee was demanded. But the training received was often nominal: the master was inclined to regard the young man as his future rival, he would therefore encourage him to be idle in order to prevent his getting too great knowledge of his customers and his methods.

London apprentices especially were by tradition idle and unruly, though people were always saying that in the good old days, before the decay of subordination, they had been dutiful and industrious. Where the system worked well was when the boy had prospects of succeeding to his master's business, often after marrying his daughter. Hogarth's crude contrast between the idle apprentice who is hanged at Tyburn, and the industrious apprentice who marries his master's daughter and becomes Lord Mayor is less remote from life than one might suppose. Francis Place records that out of twenty-one London apprentices with whom he consorted in his youth only one made his way in the world respectably. That one married his master's daughter, turned Methodist, and became a street-preacher. Of the others one at least was hanged: it is true that it was for a murder which he did not commit, but he was unable to prove an alibi because he had been engaged upon the then equally capital offence of burglary. Colquhoun, a very experienced London magistrate, called apprenticeship "a bad and immoral education." And Adam Smith said "an apprentice is likely to be idle, and almost always is so, because he has no immediate interest to be otherwise."

Idleness was more especially the temptation of the well-to-do boy. A little book called the *Apprentices' Guide* (3rd ed., 1807), much used in London as a gift for boys when they signed their indentures, speaks volumes by its petulant tone and its assumption that masters and apprentices are natural enemies. The boy is warned against absconding—" a misdemeanour of very high magnitude "; against enlisting in the Army, a course " not unfrequently adopted by idle and ill-disposed lads "; against endeavouring to do his master as much harm as possible as soon as he gets a business of his own. He is reminded of the fate of George Barnwell should he have unsuitable female acquaintances—and none is suitable but " his own relatives and the immediate connections and acquaintances of his father and mother." He is to do extra work with cheerfulness at times of necessity and he is not to resent " temporary sourness of temper " in a good master, since " business is accompanied by much care and disappointment." But in spite of such admonitions apprentices, by aping men of fashion become " frivolous and disgusting puppies," and, " it is most grievously to be lamented that there is not a more frivolous set of beings than apprentices of the present time. . . . Who can bear to see the crowd of pert young puppies who disgrace Kensington Gardens every Sunday ? " The illustration shows just such an apprentice, with just such a disgruntled master.

The lot of the poor boy was of course very different from that of such " frivolous and disgusting puppies." One was apprenticed for labour,

THE CITY 'PRENTICE AT HIS MASTER'S DOOR
Every Man's Magazine, 1771

[*face p.* 172

the other for education and admission to an exclusive trade. The master expected that the profits of the boy's work would be greater than the cost of maintaining him. At its worst this meant sheer slavery and gross ill-treatment. It was sometimes unpaid work in a blind-alley occupation, often admission to an overstocked and starving trade. Family interest or high fees, or a strict limitation of apprentices in some exclusive trades kept labour scarce and wages high. In others, apprentices were taken in great numbers as a source of cheap labour with the inevitable results: The poorer the boy the more undesirable his trade and his master. And the lot of the poor girl was likely to be far worse still.

Anyone, master or journeyman, shopkeeper or street hawker, could take an apprentice, on undertaking to feed, house and instruct the child in return for all the proceeds of its labour. The pretence of instruction in a trade was often very thin: when a little girl was bound as the drudge of a family of street hawkers living in a single room in a slum, the indentures specified that she was to be taught the art of housewifery.

Apart from obviously unpromising occupations, and apart from bad conduct on one side or the other, the possibilities of disaster were many. The man in a small way was not in a sufficiently stable position to justify a seven-years' contract. He had often no work on which an apprentice could be employed, much less taught. Apprentices were turned into the streets to pick up a living as best they could. The obligation to feed and lodge an apprentice in sickness or in health became an intolerable burden. In numberless cases apprentices were thrown on the world because their masters had gone bankrupt, were in prison, or had absconded from their creditors. Masters would sometimes retire to the workhouse or a debtors' prison, taking their apprentices with them. It occasionally happened, however, that an apprentice would be the sole support of a family whose head had thus come to grief.

Where either side broke the contract, the other could apply to Quarter Sessions to have the indentures cancelled. That is, if the master failed to teach, feed or lodge the boy, or if he administered undue correction; and on the other side, if the boy did not behave as a dutiful apprentice, there was ground for discharge. Apprentices complain that they have been deserted, turned into the streets, cruelly beaten, not taught a trade, but (for instance) forced to do housework, or made to carry out beer. One William Adams complained that instead of being taught the trade of a carpenter he had been made to drive children about at fairs for halfpence in a little cart drawn by dogs. His master, instead of providing him with clothes, had taken his clothes and pawned them. Masters complain of outrageous conduct on the part of apprentices but their complaints are less frequent. Appeals to the Sessions needed money and the help of friends, and though there are great numbers of such cases, probably the majority of unhappy apprentices simply ran away. Many boys found they had been bound for life to a trade they hated. The runaway apprentice was a sort of outlaw, unless his master could be induced to give up his indentures, and these boys were one great source of vagrancy and juvenile crime.

There were other cases which came, not before the magistrates, but before the Assizes or the Old Bailey, in which masters or mistresses were tried for doing apprentices to death by starvation or ill-treatment. Of course, things were apt to be worse in towns than in the country, scandalous conduct was more easily concealed from neighbours. But it stands to reason that to hand a child over to the complete control of someone who expects to make a profit out of its labour is not a satisfactory way of providing for it. You have only to think how it would work to-day, and then remember that manners were incomparably rougher, housing worse, excessive drinking far more common, and that very harsh treatment of the young was regarded as wholesome discipline.

The surprising thing was, not that it often worked badly, but that it sometimes worked well. The worst part of the system was that it weighted the scales so heavily against the poor and friendless child. The untaught child from a poor home or the streets was not a desirable inmate of a respectable household and only the least eligible masters were available. The worst fate of all was that of infants bound to chimney sweeps, the little climbing boys of whom Blake and Charles Kingsley have written. The very poorest London parents found they could apprentice a child to a chimney sweep much younger than to any other occupation. More than this, no apprentice fee was expected, and the master sweep was even ready to pay a sum to the parents for the services of the child, who was thus literally bought and sold. "It was a common practice," said David Porter, a remarkable master chimney-sweeper, "for parents to carry about their children to the master chimney-sweepers and dispose of them to the best bidder, as they cannot put them to any other master at so early an age." Thanks to the efforts of Jonas Hanway and others, the apprenticing of London parish children to chimney-sweepers was checked.

The lot of the parish apprentice was peculiarly hard. He was generally bound very young and had to serve for a very long term. The usual object of the parish officers was to find a master, any master, so long as he lived in some other parish, since where the first forty days of an apprenticeship was served, there a settlement or right to maintenance under the Poor Law would be gained.

Under the Elizabethan Poor Law the children of poor parents were to be apprenticed by being billeted compulsorily upon the ratepayers of the parish, to be farm servants or household servants, the boys till they were twenty-four, the girls till twenty-one or marriage; the usual age of apprenticeship was seven, but it was often younger. But as the chief desire of parish officers was to keep poor rates low, and as (after 1691) the serving of an apprenticeship in a parish for forty days was one of the ways by which a settlement was gained, it became usual to bind parish children to masters living in another parish. As Dr. Burn, the great authority on the poor laws, put it (in 1764), it was the object of the overseer to "bind out poor children apprentices, no matter to whom or to what trade, but to take especial care that the master live in another parish." And since dwellers in other parishes could not be forced to take the children it was necessary to give a fee. This was usually about £5; to a poor man, who was often a journeyman weaver, this was a fortune, and children could be useful in weaving at a very early age. The parish regarded the money as well spent—they were rid of the obligation of supporting a potential pauper. But the results for the child were too often disastrous. Let me quote what was written about this in 1738:

"A most unhappy practice prevails in most places to apprentice poor children, no matter to what master provided he lives out of the parish; if the child serves the first forty days we are rid of him for ever. The master may be a tiger in cruelty; he may beat, abuse, strip naked, starve, or do what he will to the poor innocent lad, few people take much notice, and the officers who put him out the least of any body: For they rest satisfied with the merit of having shifted him off to a neighbouring parish for three or four pounds, and the duty they owe to every poor child in the parish is no further lay'd to heart.

"The greatest part of those who now take apprentices are the most indigent and dishonest; in a word, the very dregs of the poor of England, by whom it is the fate of many a poor child, not only to be half-starved and sometimes brought up to no trade, but to be forced to thieve and steal for his master into the bargain. . . . I know a poor old weaver . . . who some time ago took a poor apprentice from another parish; he covenanted, as is usual, to teach him his trade, to provide and allow him meat, drink, apparel, etc., to save harmless and indemnify the parish whence he took him, and to give him two good new suits of wearing apparel at the end of his apprenticeship. This master had himself been several times convicted of theft, and had then actually left off his trade through weakness and old age, and as soon as the money he had with the boy was spent threw himself, apprentice and all, upon his parish." [1]

The old system of compulsory billeting of

[1] *Enquiry into the Causes of the Increase . . . of the Poor.* 1738, p. 43.

parish apprentices survived in a few places till 1844. The child began as a little drudge in some farmer's household, he became an unpaid farm-servant, and before the end of his term he probably ran away. But after 1778 the very long term of servitude for parish apprentices was reduced—they served till twenty-one instead of twenty-four. But fourteen years or so was long enough in all conscience. The long term of unpaid work in return for a bare subsistence—intended to recompense the master for the years when his work was worth little—was virtual slavery. Indeed, Blackstone defended the master's right to the perpetual service of the negro slave brought to England on the analogy of apprenticeship: he "will remain exactly in the same state of subjection for life, which every apprentice submits to for the space of seven years, and sometimes for a longer time." No wonder that apprentices so often ran away.

On the other hand, at its best, apprenticeship was an admirable training. Apprentices were sometimes the mainstay of a business, carrying it on when the master was in prison for debt. Francis Place did this, but it did not prevent him from quarrelling with his master and failing to serve out his indentures. Where apprenticeship would often work well was in such a trade as scientific instrument making, which was both a craft and a science. Jesse Ramsden, the astronomical instrument maker, who was famous throughout Europe, is described as spending his evenings by his fireside, in designing, surrounded by apprentices eager to learn. But it is worth noting that this was a trade in which apprenticeship was not compulsory—since it had not existed in 1563; in such trades apprenticeship for four years was general and the apprentice could not be used as a source of cheap labour.

Under the domestic system industry was largely carried on in the homes of the workers or in an adjoining shed. Sometimes a single room was the workplace and dwelling-place of a family, apprentice and all. Very often the journeyman or small master who had taken an apprentice for the sake of the fee had no work on which an apprentice could be employed—much less taught, and the child was turned out to pick up a living as best he could. Sometimes the master hired out his apprentice to someone else. Very often highly respectable masters extorted an amount of work which was intolerable; they would also refrain from teaching apprentices the secrets of the trade.

Most working people were affected, directly or indirectly, by apprenticeship in some form or other. It kept some trades short of labour and overstocked others. Apprenticeship was customary in some trades and in some places, especially in corporate towns. It was the common lot of the poor-law child. The small master and the journeyman taking in piecework, to do at home, often depended on the earnings of their apprentices. Nevertheless, the system was in decay. It was no longer suited to industrial conditions, the seven years' term was too long, and it was being spontaneously modified by indentures for shorter terms and by what was called outdoor apprenticeship, where the boy did not live with his master but was paid a small sum in place of board and lodging. This was technically illegal and highly disapproved of, as the ruin of all discipline, indeed, in London, it was supposed to lead straight to the gallows, but it was at least a remedy for the endless disputes about verminous beds, bad food and Sunday work. Of those who were indentured, probably the majority failed to serve out their term to the end. By the end of the century, advanced opinion was looking away from manual training and the early inuring to labour as the best introduction to life, and was looking towards some form of scholastic education.

Apprenticeship had not been kept in being by the Elizabethan Act, which had been whittled away by the judges. The old compulsory seven years' term was almost unknown among woollen-weavers, but when they became alarmed at the coming of the machine and the factory they petitioned Parliament for the enforcement of the Act which most of them had broken. Other artisans did the same, with the request that it should be extended to all trades instead of only to those in existence in 1563. The successful strikes and trade clubs which (by strikes and threats of strikes) had kept wages high in London trades during the war, relied on apprenticeship regulations as one of the means of bringing pressure to bear on their employers. Where the workmen were well organized the combination laws were quite ineffectual.

The Government had no desire to obstruct the coming of machinery or to insist on rigid barriers between trade and trade. What, it was asked in Parliament, would happen to some 30,000 gun-makers who would lose their work with the end of the war? Still less did it wish to facilitate combinations of workpeople. The Act, except in a few trades and places, had never been rigidly enforced, and its wholesale application would have been impossible.

As a result of petitions and counter-petitions, and of the attempts which had recently been made to revive apprenticeship by prosecuting "illegal workmen," the apprenticeship clauses of the Statute of Artificers of 1563 were repealed in 1814. The Committee of Manufacturers of London (which included such well-known inventors and employers as Henry Maudslay, Roger Donkin and Galloway) had no difficulty in countering the arguments of those who had petitioned for the extension of the Elizabethan Act. In answer to the contention that apprentices imbibed domestic habits and became accustomed to subordination, they quoted the recent report of the Committee on the Wool Trade, "Apprentices seem solicitous, as soon as they are able to earn workmen's wages, to render themselves obnoxious to the masters and to make it not worth while to keep them but to let them go." The petitioners had committed themselves to the absurd contention that because of the decay of apprenticeship, English manufactures had deteriorated and were " excluded from foreign markets." The London Committee retorted: " The demand for our manufactures has been so great and the obtaining of them so impossible as to have produced the most sudden and extraordinary revolution recorded in the annals of the world. The wants of the Continent have driven the hitherto victorious armies of France from the Niemen to the Vistula, from the Vistula to the Elbe, from the Elbe to the Seine." But the most interesting argument of the manufacturers and the one which could not fail to impress Parliament was that the apprenticeship clause of the Elizabethan statute gave colour to " combinations of workmen ": " Many masters are not permitted to hire their own workmen. No. The 'Shop Committee' must be applied to. They must be assured that all is right—that every workman has, as they pretend, been legally apprenticed, that is in fact that he belongs to the club. . . . They fine men also, that work for masters who conduct their business in a manner *not approved* by them. . . . Neither will they make a new article, till their Committee has decreed the price; and no member of the club dare execute it for less." Should any master resist, all the journeymen leave his shop. " But if any of them should not have been apprenticed, then is the whole artillery of the law brought out, the lawyer takes command, and whatever is the result of the action, the expenses are defrayed by 'the fund.' Nay, to such a pitch has it been carried of late in some workshops, that a labourer is not permitted to turn a grindstone. No, a regular, a legal workman at two guineas a week is the only person who is permitted to turn a stone, to sharpen a chisel or lend a hand to load a cart." This is interesting as one of many indications that the Acts against combination were very ineffective, at all events in the London district.

In any case, the raising of the question and the demand for the universal application of the Act, could have only one end. To obstruct new processes and to enforce rigid barriers between trade and trade would have been disastrous. As the employers pointed out, the Elizabethan Act could never have survived if it had been generally enforced. The apprenticeship regulations of the Elizabethan Act of 1563 were repealed. Apprenticeship became in law as well as in custom a voluntary contract, and all trades were now in the position of those which were regarded as not in existence in 1563. Coachmaking, clockmaking, mathematical instrument making, for instance—trades in which apprenticeship (though for a shorter term) had been at least as common as in those which were nominally under the Act.

In trades which were strongly organized, such as the London hatmakers, the journeymen were still able to enforce their apprenticeship rules upon the masters. Many parents, especially poor ones, still found apprenticeship the easiest way of providing for their children.

Parish apprenticeship was not affected by the repeal of the apprenticeship clauses of the Statute of Artificers, and lasted till 1844. Parish apprenticeship, many as were the abuses of the system, had this good result: parish children were the wards of the parish; they were to some extent under the supervision of the justices of the peace. When gross cases of ill-treatment came to light the justices compelled the parish officers to prosecute the masters. Thus the evils of the system became known, and in the second half of the eighteenth century there were some tentative steps for the protection of poor apprentices, especially in London and Manchester. But after this, London parishes dispatched children in waggon loads to be apprentices in cotton mills. In the then state of opinion and practice this is not to be regarded as sheer barbarity, though of course there was much carelessness and callousness. Child labour was still taken for granted. The parish officers were bound to apprentice out the waifs and strays and the children in the workhouse. The efforts of the Justices and of philanthropic individuals had more or less stopped the binding of parish children to chimney-sweeps and street hawkers.

The idea that the children of the poor should live with their parents had been as remote from the conceptions of the early eighteenth-century philanthropists as from the notions of Elizabethan statesmen. Spinning schools, workhouses and apprenticeship had all been regarded as the alternative to vice, vagrancy, crime, or at the best running wild and getting into mischief. Eighteenth-century workhouses were intended to be schools of industry and virtue, and places where some manufacture could be profitably carried on. This ideal even the best workhouse never approached. But here and there factories in the hands of some exceptional public-spirited employers actually came near it. Robert Owen's achievements at New Lanark are well known. At the apprentice-house built by Samuel Oldknow, a cotton-spinner at

Mellor, children were well fed, well housed and taught, and kindly treated. The admirable Kitty Wilkinson, whose wonderful and self-sacrificing efforts against the cholera in Liverpool have recently been commemorated by a window in Liverpool Cathedral, worked from the age of eleven to eighteen in a cotton mill at Caton, near Lancaster. She was sent to the apprentice-house there that she might have the benefit of country air. And " so kind and judicious a superintendence was exercised, that she has frequently been heard to say when relating the events of her life, ' If ever there was a Heaven upon earth it was that Apprentice House where we were brought up in such ignorance of evil.' " The apprentice-house of the Gregs at Styal where parish apprentices were fed, lodged and taught was also a place where the employers effectively considered the interests of the children.

It is probable that of all the fates possible to the untaught parish child from a poor home or the streets or the workhouse, the apprentice-house of an enlightened employer was the best that could befall him. And even the lot of the apprentice in the worst factory was probably less bad (it certainly could not have been worse) than when handed over to the tender mercies of the worst individual employer; it was at all events to the interest of the factory owner to preserve the children in health. There had been terrible cases where deaths of apprentices had seemed due to the desire of masters for a succession of apprentice fees.

In these early factories were the germs of later developments: of the State education of children (by the Act of 1801), and of the regulation of child labour—on one side by the efforts of exceptional employers, on the other through the attention which was drawn to the gross abuses in the early mills. What was new and revolutionary was that for the first time toiling children were regarded as an outrage, not as something to be admired. Children had worked for half a century in silk mills without exciting anything but admiration, and according to William Hutton their treatment had then been much harsher: by 1792, "Humanity had introduced a kinder treatment" than in his day, sixty years earlier. But the country was richer—toiling children no longer seemed the best safeguard against poverty and vagrancy. Public opinion had begun to reflect, not only the attitude of the employing classes, but also of the workers: Cotton mills when worked by water were sometimes in places where there was little work for the men of the family—this was a new development. And it was the sense of something monstrous in the factory system which directed attention to the yet more monstrous exploitation of the labour of young children.

The object-lesson of the factory directed attention to the evils of child-labour. As yet there was little feeling against child-labour in the home. Crompton, the inventor of the mule for spinning cotton, was a remarkably well-educated and highly sensitive man. He was never, it was said, either in want or in debt. His wife was an exemplary mother. Altogether the family was far removed in manners and resources, moral and material, from that of the ordinary artisan. Yet Crompton's infant son, soon after he could walk, had to cleanse cotton wool by treading on it in strong soapy water. "My mother," he says, "tucked up my petticoats and put me into the tub to tread upon the cotton at the bottom." One can imagine what was the lot of the really poor man's child. "The creatures were set to work as soon as they could crawl," said an old man, remembering the days of his youth, "and their parents were the hardest of task-masters."

CHAPTER VIII

SOME CONCLUSIONS

IT is clearly impossible to draw up a balance-sheet of the goods and ills of industrialism. There would be no agreement as to whether its ills, or goods, are increasing or decreasing. Some enthusiasts—chiefly to be found in the United States[1]—would identify industrialization and civilization. But most people would allow that its results are both good and bad. In most parts of the world industrialism has meant an advance in material civilization, a rise in the standards of living, an improved status and greater political power for the humbler classes; it has bettered health, lengthened life, lessened laborious toil, and brought with it greater leisure.

Many people would also say that industrialization has sacrificed man to the machine, has banished joy in work and destroyed craftsman-

[1] Compare *Towards Civilization*. Ed. C. A. Beard, 1930.

ship, has replaced a 'natural' by an unnatural way of life and subjected an increasing number of people to dirt, noise, and a deadening routine. Many would say that it has produced class antagonism and that under its baleful influence security and stability have been exchanged for devastating and violent fluctuations in the volume of trade and economic prosperity. There is also a general impression that in the early stages of industrialization in England, say from about 1760 to 1830, its good results had not begun to appear and its evil consequences were present in an acute form. In text-books of economic history this theory finds expression in a conventional account of "the evils of the industrial revolution."

Like most generalizations this one is far too sweeping to stand examination. Though there was much distress in this period, and especially after 1815, it was mitigated as well as aggravated by the advance of industrialism. The death-rate had declined, health had improved, many kinds of laborious toil had been made less laborious. One of the advantages claimed (about 1790) for a new method of making nails and spikes by machinery was that by the old way "it frequently happened that nail-makers were lamed in a few years and became burdensome to the parish."[1] By 1797 it was noted that since the introduction of steam Sheffield no longer abounded "in cripples and weak, deformed people" as it had when iron and steel were forged without the use of power.[2] The standard of life had risen, the poorer classes had become more articulate, better educated and better mannered. This impressed Simond, who visited England in 1810–11. "There is an ambition in parents to give a better education to their children than they have received themselves." "There is not one so low as to suffer the treatment he would have borne in former times. . . . The poor are become less ignorant and less abject." The decay of subordination was in progress—this alone would inevitably have made the workers more conscious of their wrongs and grievances without the ferment produced by the French Revolution.

The contrasts which have been drawn between the distresses of the early nineteenth century and a golden age thirty, fifty or a hundred years earlier, are coloured partly by ignorance of past conditions, partly by a new attitude to evils which had long

[1] T. Martin, *Circle of Mechanical Arts.*
[2] Housman. *Tour*, "Monthly Magazine," 1797.

existed. These had become more intolerable not only to the sufferers but to onlookers by reason of the new humanitarianism. Men's eyes were sharpened too by the growing cleavage between the landed and industrial interests: The landed classes saw the evils of the factories, the industrialists exposed the wrongs of the agricultural labourer.

In the old days poverty had been taken for granted; it had been deplored largely as the cause of an intolerable burden of poor rates. For there is nothing in the rise of poor rates at the end of the eighteenth century and after which cannot be accounted for by the growth of population, the rise in prices and, most important, the changes in administration. It leaves the question of whether there was or was not an increase in poverty unproven. To a pamphleteer writing in 1763 the two chief disadvantages of Great Britain "in Trade, Agriculture and Commerce" were, first, "that of being undersold by the French and Dutch in our principal manufactur'd goods" (a situation reversed by the time of the commercial treaty with France of 1786), and secondly, "the multiplicity of poor and idle people which infest almost every part of it and the heavy tax which is raised for the support of the same."

Many of the evils which have been regarded as the direct result of the industrial revolution were characteristic of the domestic system as of the factory system which gradually superseded it. This is true of irregular trade, with its phases of good and bad employment.[1] In the old days, child labour was limited only by the possibilities of employment—but the notion that children should be treated with tenderness was still in the future. They were regarded more as " limbs of Satan " than as " trailing clouds of glory."

The dependence of a great part of the working classes upon poor relief in old age has been regarded as a peculiar blot on the first fifty years of the nineteenth century. A blot indeed, but hardly a peculiar one. In the eighteenth century this was taken for granted and lies at the root of the unceasing war between parishes over the settlement of the poor, and the concern of the individual to establish undisputed settlement in a parish—this was his way of making provision for old age.

If there is a key to the social history of the eighteenth century it is the poor law and its administration. In the principle that every desti-

[1] See above, p. 70.

tute person had a right to maintenance, England differed, not only from continental countries but from Scotland and Ireland. Unfortunately, relief was given only in the parish where the individual had his settlement. The law of settlement was complicated, doubtful, absurd—in short the law was at its most asinine and its administration was even worse. That the labourer in general was tied to the soil by it cannot be maintained, in view of the rapid growth of towns. Constant movement was one of the results of the law: parishes had embarked on a game of inverted beggar-my-neighbour, the object being, as far as possible, to thrust all who might become a burden on the rates on to some other parish. The result was that working-people in general were regarded as potential paupers, and parishes squandered vast sums in law-suits. The consequences were complicated—they acted and reacted on every side of social life. Individual cases of hardship were innumerable. I do not think, however, that the poorer folk felt themselves humiliated by the mere fact of receiving relief. A settlement was a form of insurance. The Norfolk labourers were ready to risk their lives in defence of their liberties—that is, of their right to maintenance in their own parishes.[1] Cobbett, the son of an agricultural labourer, probably voiced his inarticulate ancestors when he said, "The poor man in England is as secure from beggary as the king upon his throne, because when he makes known his distress to the parish officers, they bestow upon him, not alms but his legal dues." This needs a great deal of qualification since the parish officers, if they could possibly dispute his settlement, would bundle him off to the other end of the country. The indignities to which the "labouring poor" were subjected gradually diminished in the course of the century. For instance, the "badging" of those receiving relief—"the parish poor"—to prevent their begging, ordered by an Act of 1697 and previously the custom of certain parishes—fell into disuse. An Act of 1795 by forbidding the removal of those "likely to become chargeable" restricted removals to those who actually applied for relief. This was a great step forward, a real measure of emancipation and reform which can be set against the disastrous order of the Berkshire justices at Speenhamland in the same year.[2]

The evils of industrialism are glaring, but they

[1] See above, p. 140. [2] See above, p. 135.

do not include a general degradation of status for working-people. Their estimation is too often based on an idealization of conditions in the good old days. It has been said that the domestic worker produced what he liked and worked when he liked. Of course he was more of a free agent in many ways than the factory worker. When he worked at home his hours were his own concern, but if he was to earn a living wage they were certainly long. Arthur Young remarked in 1767 that the Witney blanket weavers could make from 10s. to 12s. a week—high wages for weaving which was a badly paid occupation—but their hours were from four in the morning to eight at night, and in winter they worked by candle-light. This working by candle-light must have had disastrous effects on the eyesight of the workers. Hutton notes that stocking weavers all go to the workhouse "when they cannot see to work." In the Halifax district, where work was done in the employer's house, the modern factory hooter was anticipated by a horn. In summer this went at five in the morning, in winter at six, while the evening horn went at eight.

Then there is the question of design and craftsmanship. Many people seem to assume that the hand-loom weavers of the old days were in the position of the modern hand-loom weaver. It would be as reasonable to suppose that an Elizabethan alehouse resembled the modern inn or tea-shop which calls itself 'Ye Olde Englyshe Hostelrye.' The weaver as a rule was achieving mass-production by dint of unremitting bodily effort. He worked to a standard, often on warps given out by his employer. The element of design did not even come into the work of the Spitalfields brocade weavers though these were highly skilled men. The employers, who were usually the mercers, gave out the patterns sometimes copied from French materials, sometimes supplied by the professional pattern-drawers of Spitalfields. Before the adoption of the Jacquard loom the pattern was produced by a boy—called a draw-boy—who pulled the threads which made the design while the weaver threw the shuttle. But this was excessively laborious and was often too much for the boy to the interruption of the weaver's work.[1] The theory that the domestic weaver felt a creator's pride in his work started, I think, in the days of Ruskin and William Morris. Doubtless some did—pride in work, mercifully, is not uncommon—but it seems

[1] See M. D. George, *London Life*, pp. 177, 183.

unlikely that the average weaver toiling hour after hour, throwing the shuttle backwards and forwards on work which was monotonous and exhausting, had the reactions which would satisfy a modern enthusiast for peasant arts.

When we think of joy in work as being the happy lot of the domestic worker of the past it is as well to remember Francis Place's account of the 'sickening aversion' to his work which periodically overcame every working man, and drove him to idleness and drink, a phenomenon which explains a good deal of the social history of the eighteenth century and which is to be explained at least in part by the normal monotony of work.

One reason for the belief that in the days before machinery the average worker was a highly skilled craftsman lies in the fact that the insistence on a seven years' apprenticeship is supposed to show that it took seven years to learn a trade. Of course those journeymen and masters who were anxious at the beginning of the nineteenth century to preserve compulsory apprenticeship maintained that this was so. But apprenticeship had other motives, varying from trade to trade: to restrict admission to it, or alternatively, to supply cheap labour; it was a way of providing a maintenance for children, a means of securing a right to a settlement. (Lord Mansfield said that if this last motive disappeared he thought indentures of apprenticeship would disappear too.)

In most trades the apprentice, long before his term was out, was expected to do a man's work for his master's benefit. That there was excellent craftsmanship in the old days, much of which has been superseded by machinery, no one would deny. But there is also much skilled craftsmanship to-day, and it would be rash to assert that there is now less demand in industry for the qualities of intelligence and resourcefulness or even manual skill than in the old days. One can compare, as an example, the work of the plumber in the early eighteenth and twentieth centuries as highly typical of their periods. The old plumber's work was the casting of lead. He covered roofs, made pipes and cisterns, which were often beautifully decorated when they were for grand houses, he cast, though he did not design, the little garden statues in lead which were so popular. His work was excessively laborious and very unhealthy as he was exposed to lead-poisoning in an acute form. The results of his labours were often beautiful. The modern plumber (jokes apart) is a highly skilled workman with a knowledge of mechanics. He also is a craftsman, and his work is probably at least as interestingly varied as that of his namesake in the old days, though its æsthetic interest is less.

That an enormous amount of laborious toil has disappeared with the coming of the machine is obvious, yet often seems to be forgotten by those who regard the pre-machine age as a paradise for workpeople. De Quincey, visiting Derby in 1772, noted that besides the great Derby silk mill, there were smaller mills, some worked by water, others by " the pressure of children, &c., in a large wheel, similar to that of a common crane." A form of child labour which no one appears to have thought unsuitable. " Turning a wheel " was a process needed in many industries, and it was particularly the lot of children[1] and blind people. The craftsman of the good old days is remembered, but the majority, who were labourers, are often forgotten. If the craftsman had a superior status it was because he belonged to a privileged minority.

Besides the legend of regular, easy and congenial work in the good old days it is sometimes said that strikes and labour disputes were rare. Of course

[1] See above, p. 146.

where the transition from journeyman to master was easy they would be less frequent, and where the workers lived in scattered cottages combination would be more difficult. In 1836 Gaskell, who is one of the chief authorities for the evils of the early factories, drew an idyllic picture, or what he regarded as an idyllic picture, of the domestic worker of the recent past, comparing him very unfavourably with the Manchester factory worker of his own day. The comparison is very instructive. "In the old days," he says, "there was a steady and equable flow of occupation. . . ." This was certainly not true in general.[1] Children did not work before fourteen or sixteen, before that they learned subordination in the home. (This again is far from the truth, though instances here and there might have been discoverable.) "The distinctions of rank were then in full force." (Perhaps relatively true, as compared with 1836, though of course they had long been crumbling as Dr. Johnson was so painfully aware.) The domestic worker could "seldom read freely or write at all." His was "an ignorance of almost everything but the common arts of life," but he went to church or chapel with exemplary regularity. (True or false,

[1] See above, pp. 68 ff.

the significant thing is that to Gaskell this was highly satisfactory.) He had a sluggish mind in an active body. His wages were low, but they were sufficient for his simple wants. And, he says, " combinations, strikes and labour disputes were unknown." (This is demonstrably false.) On the other hand, the artisan of 1836 has an active mind in a sickly body. " He shows a very high order of intelligence, seeking his amusement in the newspaper, the club, the political union, or the lecture-room, looking for his stimulus in gin and beer shops. . . ." The modern system of the factory, affords " every facility for secret cabal and co-operative union among work-people." It communicates " intelligence and energy to the vulgar mind," while liberal wages supply " the pecuniary sinews of contention." Gaskell, of course, is speaking of the élite of the Manchester workmen. The old domestic worker, he asserts, knew nothing of " clubs for raving politicians or combinations which could place him in opposition to his employer—but he was respectful to his superiors and fulfilled his contracts to the letter." As a matter of fact, even the Lancashire domestic weaver,[1] with his comparative isolation and low pay, managed to

[1] Cf. G. W. Daniels, *The Early English Cotton Industry*, 1920.

combine and to strike. The best comment on Gaskell's assertion is to be found in a speech of Lord Mansfield, the famous Chief Justice, when he had to deal with strikers at the County Assizes in 1758. He spoke of "great disturbances in Lancashire, occasioned by several thousands having left their work—and entered into combinations for raising their wages . . . formed themselves into a committee . . . and established boxes and fixed stewards in every township for collecting money for such weavers as should by their Committee be ordered to leave their masters, and made other dangerous and illegal regulations . . . they had insulted and abused several weavers who had refused to join in their scheme and continued to work, and had dropt incendiary letters with threats to masters. . . ." The important thing to notice is that these strikers are Gaskell's dutiful and contented domestic weavers to whom combinations and strikes were unknown.

Labour disputes were certainly less common among the domestic weavers in the North than elsewhere, but strikes took place even in Lancashire and the West Riding. In the South they were far more frequent and, as one might expect, they were particularly common in London. They were considered as one of the chief handicaps to English trade in competition with foreign rivals.

It is evident from Gaskell's diatribe that he resents the new class-conscious, politically-minded working man. That something of value and charm was lost with the disappearance of the old state of things is certain.

Something of it can be learnt from Bamford's *Early Days*, always remembering that Bamford was a romantic and was personally and socially in a favourable position as compared with the average Lancashire weaver. Whether the balance was a loss or gain depends upon the standpoint of the observer: to Gaskell it was sheer loss (but then his knowledge of the earlier period was sketchy); to Francis Place it was almost equally unmixed gain. He regarded the advance of the working man in political knowledge and activity which dated from the French Revolution as the chief cause of a great social advance in manners and morals: "Look even to Lancashire. Within a few years a stranger walking through their towns was 'touted,' i.e. hooted, and an outcomling was sometimes pelted with stones. 'Lancashire brute' was the common and appropriate appellation. Until very lately it would have been dangerous to have assembled five hundred of them on any occasion. Bakers and butchers would at least have been plundered. Now a hundred thousand people may be collected together and no riot ensue, and why ?" His answer is, the movement for political reform: "the people have an object, the pursuit of which gives them importance in their own eyes, elevates them in their own opinion. . . ."

This brings us to one of the most vital points in our judgment of the (so-called) Industrial Revolution, did it bring distress and degradation to the workers or did it mean a step forwards ? That it was a real advance in social status I think can hardly be doubted. That it was a material advance statistics of health and wages show. That there were victims of this advance, as of others, is of course certain. Among them were (conspicuously) the hand-loom weavers and (perhaps) the agricultural labourers. But it must not be forgotten that the agricultural labourer had long been "the lowest member, the feet of the body politic." That by the great Elizabethan code, anyone without means of subsistence could be forced to work for the farmer, and that compulsory apprenticeship to husbandry was the lot of the children of the destitute.

The new regime of the machine and the factory inherited from the past certain deeply-rooted beliefs and customs. These included the custom of child labour at a very early age and the belief that it was socially valuable. The belief rapidly vanished under the pressure of the factory system. Then, too, the belief in the dangerous consequences of high wages was deeply ingrained.[1] Antagonism between capital and labour, employer and employed, or in the old term, master and man, was no new thing. Disputes were usually accompanied by much personal bitterness and violence. Francis Place, from his own experience as a journeyman under the domestic system, taking home work given out by his employer, had the most pessimistic views on the relationship between employer and employed. Justice, he thought, would never be done to the worker, " because it is not the habit of men to care for others beneath them in rank, and because they who employ them will probably never fail to look grudgingly on the pay they are compelled to give them for their services, the very notion of which produces an inward hatred of them, a feeling so common, that it is visible in the countenance and manners in nearly every one who has to pay

[1] See above, p. 80.

either journeymen, labourers or servants."[1] The possibilities for antagonism and injury in the old domestic system are well displayed (from the worker's standpoint) in the ballad of *The Clothier's Delight.*[2] Combinations to raise wages were not only thought to be pernicious but were crimes in the eyes of the law. The Combination Act of 1800 (which replaced the Act of 1799) was only the last, and probably the least effective, as it was the mildest in the penalties it imposed, of a long series of Acts penalizing combination, all repealed in 1824.[3]

These things were not calculated to make transition less difficult. They are indeed often thought to be a product of the new regime. And the new order found itself in violent conflict, not only with the custom of irregular hours of work—excessive toil compensated for by hours or days of leisure—but with the workers' age-long hatred and dread of machines. This dread was the more natural since the old order had been based on a rigid division between occupations hardening at times almost into a system of caste: with its standard of a

[1] G. Wallas, *Life of Place*, p. 14.

[2] See above, p. 66.

[3] See M. D. George, *The Combination Laws Reconsidered*, "Econ. Journal," May 1927.

seven years' apprenticeship it had stood, in theory at least, for the absolute non-fluidity of labour.

Historians have seen in the unrest which followed 1815 and lasted more or less till 1848 evidence of the worsening of conditions—if not material then moral and æsthetic.[1] But is organized unrest and discontent usually the result of a worsening of conditions ? Surely it comes with ill-adjusted and painful progress—when a class or a people has made a material or intellectual advance which has not been adequately recognized in the political or social sphere, or when political achievements have outstripped economic status. One thinks of English peasants in 1381, of American colonists after 1763, of the French bourgeoisie before 1789—not to speak of more modern instances. The organized discontent after 1815 (unlike wild outbursts of rioting) is not in itself evidence of an oppressed and poverty-stricken people. And it was most rife among those sections of the workers who were the best paid and the most intelligent, those who, to quote Gaskell, had " the pecuniary sinews of con-

[1] Cf. J. L. and B. Hammond, *The Age of the Chartists*, 1930.

tention " as well as the " intelligence and energy " which came from " the modern system," and which he thought so demoralizing to ' the vulgar mind.' As Dr. Johnson said, " gold and silver destroy feudal subordination."

APPENDIX

THE following figures[1] bring into comparison Gregory King's estimate of the population and wealth of England and Wales at the end of the seventeenth century with that of Colquhoun (based on the Census of 1801 and the Poor Law Returns of 1803). Colquhoun first takes the classes as given by King and then adds those classes which the social and economic changes of a century had brought into importance. The most noteworthy addition is the new class of " manufacturers employing capital in all branches, wool, cotton, flax, hemp, silk, hats, leather, paper, books, glass, pottery, iron, steel, gold, silver, and other metals : gunpowder, painters' colours, dye stuffs, &c., ale, beer, porter, distilled liquors, sweets, soap, candles, salt, tobacco, &c." Individuals in this class of course had existed in King's day, but their number, wealth and importance was a new development.

Perhaps the chief interest in the comparison lies in the classes whom King regarded as " decreasing the wealth of the nation."[2] Colquhoun classes as paupers those who received help from the rates while their own earnings averaged £10 a family. Of these there are 260,179 families (1,040,716 souls) and they receive from the poor rates an average of rather over £16 a family in the course of a year. The self-supporting

[1] From P. Colquhoun, *Treatise on Indigence*, 1806.

[2] See above, page 4.

labourers in husbandry, the poorest class apart from common soldiers and vagrants, he estimated at 340,000 families (1,530,000 souls) who earned annually, "including the earnings of females," £31 a family. King, a century earlier, regarded all labourers as earning less than they consumed. But in the meantime the poor rates of the country had risen from about £700,000 to £4,267,000: "It is probable that the indigent of the present period (including all descriptions) are not only upon the whole less moral; but also, from more dissolute habits, less frugal, than a century ago; and there is no doubt also that they experience more attention and much greater assistance . . . yet, notwithstanding the enormous sums expended it has been already seen . . . how much the evil has increased, and also the mass of turpitude which envelops the chief part of the indigent."

As a London magistrate, with a knowledge of London crime, there is reason to think that Colquhoun exaggerated the "mass of turpitude." In any case, of course, these figures are estimates only[1]: neither he nor King can claim to approach accuracy, but in Colquhoun's words, he makes "an attempt to exhibit a general view of Society, and to estimate the National Income . . . from different sources comprising Landed Property, Mines and Minerals, the Public Funds, Agriculture, Commerce, and Shipping; Manufactures, Inland Trade and Professional and Manual Labour, and Colonial, East India and foreign Incomes."

[1] That is, as regards earnings and income. The poor-law returns, too, were defective in many ways, and the census of 1801 was not accurate.

Gregory King's Estimate, 1696, "calculated for the Year 1688," based on the Hearth Tax, etc.

No. of families		Heads per family.	No. of persons.	Yearly income per family.	Yearly income & expense per head. Inc.	Exp.
				£ s.	£ s.	£ s.
160	Temporal lords . .	40	6,400	2,800	70	60
26	Spiritual lords . . .	20	520	1,300	65	55
800	Baronets . . .	16	12,800	880	55	51
600	Knights	13	7,800	650	50	46
3,000	Esquires	10	3,000	450	45	42
12,000	Gentlemen . . .	8	96,000	280	35	32 10
5,000	Persons in offices . .	8	40,000	240	30	27
5,000	,, ,, . .	6	30,000	120	20	18
2,000	Merchants and traders by sea	8	16,000	400	50	40
8,000	Merchants and traders by land	6	48,000	200	33	28
10,000	Persons in the Law . .	7	70,000	140	20	17
2,000	Clergymen . . .	6	12,000	60	10	9
8,000	,, ...	5	40,000	45	9	8
40,000	Freeholders (better sort) .	7	280,000	84	12	11

000	,, (lesser sort)	5	700,000	50	10	9 2
000	Farmers	5	750,000	44	8 15	8 10
000	Persons in sciences and liberal arts	5	80,000	60	12	11 10
000	Shopkeepers and tradesmen	4½	180,000	45	10	9 10
000	Artisans and handicrafts	4	240,000	40	10	9 10
000	Naval officers	4	16,000	80	20	18
000	Military officers	4	16,000	60	15	14
ersons increasing the wealth of the country			2,675,500			
000	Common seamen	3	150,000	20	7	7 10
000	Labouring people and out-servants	3½	1,275,000	15	4 10	4 12
000	Cottagers and paupers	3¼	1,300,000	6 10	2	2 5
000	Common soldiers	2	70,000	14	7	7 10
			2,795,000			
	Vagrants	(No families)	30,000	2	2	3
ersons decreasing the wealth of the country			2,825,000			

P. Colquhoun's Estimate Based on the Census Returns of 1801 and the Pauper Returns of 1803.[1]

No. of families.		Persons in each family.	Aggregate of persons.	Yearly income per family, averaged.	Aggregate income of each rank.
				£	£
287	Temporal peers and peeresses, including princes of the blood	25	7,175	8,000	2,296,000
26	Bishops	15	390	4,000	104,000
540	Baronets	15	8,100	3,000	1,620,000
350	Knights	10	3,500	1,500	525,000
6,000	Esquires	10	60,000	1,500	9,000,000
20,000	Gentlemen and ladies living on incomes	8	160,000	700	14,000,000
2,000	Persons in higher civil offices (state and revenue)	7	14,000	800	1,600,000
10,500	Persons in lesser civil offices (state and revenue)	5	52,500	200	2,100,000
2,000	Eminent merchants, bankers, etc. . .	10	20,000	2,600	5,200,000
13,000	Lesser merchants trading by sea . .	7	91,000	800	10,400,000
11,000	Persons of the Law (judges, barristers, attorneys, clerks, etc.)	5	55,000	350	3,850,000
1,000	Eminent clergymen	6	6,000	500	500,000
10,000	Lesser clergymen	5	50,000	120	1,200,000
40,000	Freeholders of the better sort . .	5½	220,000	200	8,000,000
120,000	Lesser freeholders	5	600,000	90	10,800,000
160,000	Farmers	6	960,000	120	19,200,000
16,300	Liberal arts and sciences (medical, literary and fine arts)	5	81,500	260	4,238,000
74,500	Shopkeepers and tradesmen	5	372,500	150	11,175,000
445,726	Artisans, handicrafts and labourers employed in manufactures, building, and works of every kind	4½	2,005,767	55	24,514,930

3,000	Nava officers, marine officers, surgeons, etc.	5	15,000	149	1,043,000
5,000	Military officers, including surgeons .	5	25,000	139	1,815,900
50,000	Common soldiers, including non-commissioned officers and militia	—	200,000	29	5,510,000
38,175	Marines and seamen in the Navy and revenue service	—	150,000	38	4,940,000
67,099	Seamen in the Merchant Service, fisheries, rivers, canals, etc.	—	299,663	40	7,200,000
40,000	Labouring people in husbandry, including earnings of the females	4½	1,530,000	31	10,540,000
40,000	Labouring people in mines, canals, etc. .	4½	130,000	40	1,600,000
60,179	Paupers producing from their own labours in miscellaneous employments . .	4	1,040,716	10	2,601,790
	And receiving from parochial rates :				4,267,000
	Vagrants, gipsies, rogues and vagabonds, thieves, swindlers, coiners of base money, in and out of prison, and common prostitutes, including wives and children	—	222,000	10	2,222,000

[1] These categories correspond to those of King.

REMARKS. " Incomes . . . are not considered in every occasion as arising merely from one, but various es ; although chiefly in the case of the landholder from rents, and in the case of the merchants from nerce. There are certainly more freeholders than these stated as such, since, in the present times, almost y person who is in any degree opulent, is also of this class.

Many of the freeholders . . . may be considered as increasing the number of farmers.

All persons who employ capital in fabricating or finishing for sale or consumption any article *whatever* iere ranked as manufacturers.

Others who are employed in these various branches are classed as working artisans.

PERSONS NOT INCLUDED IN GREGORY KING'S ESTIMATE

No. of families.		Persons in each family.	Aggregate of persons	Yearly income per family averaged. £	Aggregate income. £
1	The Sovereign, household, etc. . .	50	50	200,000	200,000
50,000	Shipowners, letting ships for freights only	5	25,000	500	2,500,000
25,000	Manfacturers employing capital in all branches, wool, cotton . . .[1] . .	6	150,000	800	20,000,000
500	Principal warehousemen selling by wholesale	6	3,000	800	400,000
300	Persons employing capital in building and repairing ships and crafts, etc .	6	1,800	700	210,000
25,000	Persons employing capital as tailors, mantua-makers, milliners, etc., including Army clothiers	5	125,000	150	3,750,000
5,000	Persons employing professional skill and capital as engineers, surveyors, master-builders of houses	5	25,000	200	1,000,000
30,000	Clerks and shopmen to merchants, manufacturers, shopkeepers, etc. etc . .	5	150,000	75	6,750,000
2,500	Clergymen regularly ordained, dissenting from the established Church . .	5	12,500	120	300,000
500	Persons educating youth in universities and chief schools	4	2,000	600	300,000
20,000	Persons employed in the education of youth of both sexes and generally employing some capital . . .	6	120,000	150	3,000,000

500	Persons employed in theatrical pursuits and attached to theatres and concerts as musicians, etc.	4	2,000	200	400,000
800	Hawkers and pedlars, duffers and others, with and without licences	5	4,000	40	100,000
2,000	Persons confined in prisons for debt	5	10,000	25	87,750
40	Persons keeping houses for lunatics	10	400	500	20,000
....	Lunatics, etc., in public and private asylums (2,500 individuals)	—	2,500	30	75,000
0,000	Innkeepers and publicans	5	250,000	100	5,000,000
2,000	Military, naval and medical half-pay officers	5	10,000	45	180,675
0,500	{ Pensioners of Chelsea College, in and out. Pensioners of Greenwich Hospital, in and out. Pensioners of the Chest at Chatham }	4	70,500	10	305,000
	Receiving besides from labour	—	—	10	305,000
0,000	Persons included in the various families above mentioned who have incomes from the funds and other sources, including also trustees for orphans, minors and charitable institutions	—	—	—	5,055,955
	Totals: 1,905.823 Families in 1801.		9,343,561 Population, including soldiers and seamen.		£222,000,000 Total yearly income of the Nation.

[1] See page 213.

INDEX